Positive Legacy

How to live a life of meaning and impact

Ambrose Enuma

ISBN: 978-978-998-134-2

Pente Publishing

Blk A, Suite 53, Alausa Shopping Mall,
131, Obafemi Awolowo Way, Ikeja, Lagos, Nigeria

www.pentepublishing.com

P.O. Box 16413, Ikeja PO

Lagos, Nigeria.

DEDICATION

To God—all the glory belongs for all-round enablement to complete this project; to my wife—Bridget—for love, belief, and unalloyed support; to my wonderful children—Cherish, Donald, and Eunice—for constantly raising the bar of success and putting me on my toes continually; to everyone in a position of influence—I pray that you will find the right guidance; to those unsure of life's purpose—I earnestly hope that you will swiftly find your bearing; and to my bosom friend—Adolphus Aduku—who almost paid the ultimate price for my sake.

CONTENTS

ACKNOWLEDGMENTS

Inputs from several quarters melded to realize this project. If I omitted you in my mention, please accept my apology; it does not diminish your effort towards this project's completion.

My gratitude goes to Adewale Babalola, for going through the first draft of the manuscript—your kind review was a morale booster; Benson Eluma, for being such a great critique that impacted on the final output; Mrs Emilia Adeniya, for creating time during the ever-busy Yuletide period to look through the work and in picking out a few niggles; Samson Ogunyowa, for support during the second phase; Celestine Enuma—my big brother, for enthusiasm during the finishing stages; Rita Oyibo—my unflagging cheerleader; Pastor Bamidele Akinyemi, for always being supportive; and Elder Waheed Akinyemi, for locational support.

Numerous online sources were consulted during the quest for information; several have been acknowledged in the bibliography. However, a handful may not have been mentioned because of the width and depth of research, the indirect nature of the information they provided, or to avoid repetition. Nonetheless, the information gleaned from them impacted the outcome of this book.

INTRODUCTION

I designed Positive Legacy in a tripod-like fashion; it has a limb in history, another within the present, and the third in the future. When I talk to young people, I am alarmed that they engross themselves in the present with limited attention to the future implications of their present actions and near-total oblivion of the past aside from glimpses through movies that may not tell the entire story. Engaging the matured does not appear to be encouraging either; a good number of them have only a vague and haphazard recollection of important events and personalities that shaped our world. The realization of the yawning gaps informed the direction of this book; please bear with me if I bore you with some historical details—it is deliberate. You deserve to know because I am convinced that past information is of great use in shaping the present and the future.

While ensuring that I did not depart from the subject, legacy, I made a conscious effort to bring history to the fore, and at the same time, make it engaging: I hope I achieved it.

After reading this book, below are my expectations:
- You will develop a positive legacy consciousness
- For the curious mind, it will motivate you to seek more information concerning past events
- You will learn how to take advantage of positive legacy opportunities

- You will have a clearer picture of the pathway you are currently on in terms of legacy and have a good insight into the expected outcome
- You will have the knowledge, motivation, and courage to change your path where necessary
- You will feel the stimulation to positively impact our world and make it a better place for everyone.

I had a broad audience in mind while putting this book together; it cuts across all ages (except the very young ones), gender, religion, and social class. Doing a book that can accommodate such a vast and diverse group is by no means an inconsiderable task.

Finally, one of the intents of this book is to develop a foundation for continuous discussions and engagements on the subject to build knowledge around the topic for the greater good of humankind. Plans are in place to push this subject beyond the confines of this book and create a forum where everyone can contribute meaningfully towards the development of the subject matter.

Ambrose Enuma
April 2022

1 UNDERSTANDING LEGACY

"Carve your name on hearts, not tombstones. A legacy is etched into the minds of others and the stories they share about you."

………..Shannon Alder

Legacy is a word that is often in use but not as explored as I believe it should. The subject affects everyone, irrespective of age, gender, race, or creed. We will start this exciting journey by first examining the dictionary meanings of legacy; thereafter, drill it down to the direction of legacy this book addresses. I welcome you on board as we embark on this enthralling journey together.

Review of dictionary meanings of legacy

Merriam-Webster dictionary has five definitions of legacy; the first three are in noun form, and the last two are in adjective form. A sixth definition is a noun form from Longman's Dictionary of Contemporary English.

i) A gift by will, especially of money or other personal property
ii) Something transmitted by or received from an ancestor or predecessor or the past
iii) A candidate for membership in an organization
iv) Of, relating to, or being a previous or outdated computer system
v) Of, relating to, associated with, or carried over from an earlier time, technology, and business
vi) Something that happens or exists because of things that happened earlier.

Definition one relates to physical assets passed from a deceased to another, usually an heir, relative, or public institution. It relates to the legacy this book addresses, but the addition is that legacy addresses more than the passage of tangible assets from one person to another.

Definition two addresses legacy in an unqualified form of what was bequeathed by predecessors or ancestors. It gives one room to qualify the bequest; this definition partly addresses the legacy under discussion.

Definition three addresses certain privileges that one is entitled to through a close relative who had or still has a relationship with an organization. For instance, a parent being an alumnus of an organization (company or school) gives the child a distinct edge in being accepted into that organization, especially if the referenced person has an excellent track record. This definition partly addresses the legacy under discussion.

Definition four relates directly to outdated computers that are not in use but kept for reference or research purposes. This book does not address this kind of legacy directly. However, if I stretch the definition in relative terms, it could refer to an old action taken by somebody that could be a reference point in the future.

Definition five refers to actions or activities of a person in earlier times having an impact in the present time. This definition addresses the legacy under discussion because it opens it to a wide range of effects.

As mentioned earlier, definition six is from Longman's Dictionary of Contemporary English; it looks at legacy from the perspective of cause and effect. The cause happened in a previous period when the result was felt; it affects the present and possibly continues to impact the future. This definition primarily covered the legacy I will be addressing in this book.

Combining all the six definitions above, a comprehensive definition of legacy can be derived.

Before I come up with a definition, let me trace the word's root. Legacy has its origin in the Latin word *Legare,* meaning to bequeath. Bequeath means to pass something on, leave something behind. Most bequests connote direct giving. For example, passing on assets to relatives. However, the legacy under discussion extends beyond that because direct giving is more related to tangible assets, and legacy covers both tangible and intangible assets and liabilities. Legacy has another Latin root: *legatus* (ambassador, envoy, sent, and deputy); nonetheless, *Legare* is more relevant to this topic.

I view legacy as *"quantifiable and unquantifiable assets, liabilities, or an event that a person, group of persons, an organization(s), or people group leave(s) behind for all stakeholders."*

Quantifiable assets imply those positive, tangible resource(s) or benefit(s) left behind by the predecessor. For instance, a father could bequeath houses, money, and companies to his children, relatives, or the government. Likewise, a good government can bequeath excellent infrastructures such as good roads, bridges, and edifices to its citizens.

Unquantifiable assets for individuals could be a good reputation, impeccable character, good networks, and relationships. In government circles, unquantifiable assets are good international relations, great institutions, and a good reputation.

In terms of quantifiable liabilities, parents could bequeath unpaid debts and diseases to their children, and a government can bequeath debt and dilapidated infrastructure to its citizens as well.

In the case of unquantifiable liabilities, one could bequeath strife, notorious name, illiteracy, and negative character to his successors. Concerning governments, an unquantifiable liability could be in the form of strained international relations, unpleasant reputation, poverty, bad governance, nepotism, internal strife, and corruption of the citizens.

Regarding an event, one should look at the legacy from the perspective of who is involved. For the root legacy (the origin of the legacy), it is either an asset or a liability. It will also be either an asset or liability for the direct relatives of a root legacy, but for beneficiaries that have no familial relationship with the bequeather: it is primarily assets. It is viewed as an event if the referenced person(s) or people group are neither connected nor directly impacted by the consequences of the legacy.

By stakeholders, I mean person(s) directly or indirectly affected by another's actions or inactions.

A second perspective one can look at legacy is *"what comes to your mind when the name of a person, an organization, or a country is mentioned."* For example, if you hear Adolf Hitler, World War II comes to your consciousness; Eron, creative accounting; and Brazil, soccer. The event that comes to your consciousness is the legacy of the referenced person or organization.

Interestingly, a predecessor can bequeath legacy through an earlier action or inaction. For instance, some families have become the ruling class in some countries because their forebearers had early education, while others did not embrace it. The uneducated families could remain subservient to the educated families whose early education propelled them to become the ruling class. It is safe to say that the illiteracy prevalent in some developing countries is a legacy of the forebearers that continues to hurt their offspring. Also, some families are currently enjoying the gift of fortunes left behind by their forebearers. A reference case is the Rockefeller family; the descendants continue to enjoy the wealth left behind by their progenitor, John D. Rockefeller.

Categories of legacy

One can delineate person(s) or organization(s) into three distinct legacy categories. The impact and the sustainability of the legacy determine the categorization:

i)   No legacy
ii)   Temporary legacy
iii)   Permanent legacy

It is no legacy if there is nothing of note associated with the person or organization. It may be challenging to say that some persons or organizations do not have any legacy because I believe that one's life should at least impact somebody or something, whether negatively or positively. However, the legacy may not be noteworthy; the referenced person or organization likely lived a mundane lifestyle, in conformity with societal norms, and was afraid to question the status quo or make the bold steps to see his idea(s) through. People who have no legacy are usually conformists that rarely want to ruffle any feather; they go through life's journey largely unnoticed and easily forgotten after death. Sadly, a sizeable number of people fall into the no-legacy category.

Persons or organizations with temporary legacies made attempts and did something of note, but the achievement(s) did not last for long. Over time, more enduring legacies overshadowed their legacies. People who fall into the temporary legacy category could be scientists that started research, made significant progress, but the credit for the last discovery and patenting was ascribed to somebody else.

In respect of permanent legacies, their actions stood the test of time. From the previous instance, people who made the last discovery and got credit for it have permanent legacies.

In 1903, American-born entrepreneurs, the Wright brothers, Wilbur and Orville, designed, built, and successfully tested a controllable and sustainable heavier than air aircraft in the history of airplane development. It is their success that led to modern-day aircraft. However, before their successful test, several aeronautical pioneers made a series of developments that the Wright brothers built on. Between 1890 and 1897, different scientists, aviators, and aeronautical engineers attempted to improve the aircraft. French inventor Clement Ader designed and built Ader Éole in 1890, German aviator Otto Lilienthal designed and built the Lilienthal Standard Glider in 1894, American civil engineer Octave Chanute designed and built the Chanute Glider in 1896, American astronomer Samuel Langley designed and constructed the Pilcher Hawk in 1896, English aviator Percy Sinclair designed and developed the Pilcher in 1896, and Clement Ader designed and constructed Ader Avion III in 1897. The scientists, aviators, and engineers made different improvements in the above inventions, but each aircraft had different challenges. As each development improved, it covered up the previous progress.

Inputs in aviation in the period cut across four countries (The United States, France, Germany, and Britain) and two continents (Europe and America). I can classify the earlier developments between 1890 and 1897 into temporary legacies, while the achievements of the Wright brothers fall into the permanent legacy category.

2 TYPES AND LEVELS OF LEGACY

"We will be known forever by the track we leave"

.... Native America Dakota Proverb

Types of legacy

Legacy can be classified into two types: positive or negative. Positive legacy is desirable and affects everyone connected to it. For instance, anyone bearing or having a familial relationship with Mandela is privileged to enjoy some form of goodwill, especially in South Africa. Mandela left behind a positive legacy regarding the apartheid struggle. If it were a negative legacy, everyone with a familial connection to him would also bear the accompanying burden.

A positive legacy bestows positive vibes on anyone associated with it; it opens doors of opportunities and grants benefits that some may argue are undeserved. Suppose there is a black sheep in Mandela's family, he will still enjoy certain liberties from the South African society and government because of Nelson Mandela's positive legacy status. In contrast, a person with a similar reputation from a nondescript background will face challenges from the law and society.

On the flip side is negative legacy; this happens when one's name, family, or organization is associated with notoriety: Adolf Hitler, Joseph Stalin, Idi Amin, and Pablo Escobar. It is usually discomforting for those directly related to the names; some had to change them to avoid embarrassment. I can imagine how it would have looked like in the 1950s to be a Hitler; I believe it would have been a challenge to get employed, do business, get married, or associate freely. A name change might be an easy option; however, it does not solve the problem because the negative vibes will continue to resonate. I liken a name change to a large extended family that went on a cruise and ran into turbulence; you quietly take a life-raft and escape with your immediate family leaving your extended family in limbo. I believe one can explore better options to save the entire family. I will discuss the options in a later chapter—*how to repair negative legacy.*

Levels of legacy

One can also group legacy in terms of levels. By levels, I am looking at either the source or the spread of the legacy. Levels of legacy include personal or root, family, indirect/associative, city, tribal, regional, national, and continental legacy. One of the descriptions of legacy is what readily comes to your mind when the name of a person, city, region, country, continent, or organization is mentioned. The mental picture could be positive or negative depending on the preconceived perceptions the name generates.

1) *Personal or root legacy*
Legacies are usually directly linked to a person, groups of people, or an organization—the originator(s) of the legacy. Whether a positive or

negative legacy, somebody's action, inaction, or position created it. The personal or root legacy is usually the person(s) that readily come to one's mind when the legacy in question comes to the fore. Examples include World War II, Adolf Hitler; Holocaust of the Jews during World War II, Adolf Hitler; peaceful agitation for human rights in the United States, Martin Luther King Jr.; agitation against the apartheid regime in South Africa, Nelson Mandela; the Medellin drug cartel, Pablo Escobar; the Cali drug cartel, Rodriguez Orejuela brothers; and Black Lives Matter Movement, George Floyd.

Several players may have occasioned the legacy in some cases, but there is usually a face or a name attached to the legacy. For instance, during the struggle against apartheid regime in South Africa, there were various participants: individuals such as Albert Luthuli, Ahmed Kathrada, Amina Cachalia, Denis Goldberg, Govan Mbeki, Helen Joseph, Joe Slovo, Lilian Ngoyi, Nelson Mandela, Oliver Tambo, Robert Sobukwe, Steve Biko, Walter Sisulu and a host of others; associations such as African National Congress (ANC), Congress of South African Students (COSAS), Federation of South African Women (FEDSAW), Mass Democratic Movement (MDM), National Education Crisis Committee (NECC), Pan-African Congress (PAC), South Africa Council of Churches (SACC), South African Congress of Democrats (SACOD), South Africa Congress of Trade Union (SACTU), South African Indian Congress (SAIC), South African Students Congress (SASC), South Africa Student Movement (SASM), South African Students Organization (SASO); countries such as Jamaica through banning of South African passport holders from entering the country, India—one of the first countries to oppose, severe relations, and impose both political and economic sanctions against the apartheid regime as well as mobilize other countries to follow suit, Nigeria through the boycott of Commonwealth games in 1978 and 1986, Zambia, Tanzania, and the Soviet Union that supported militarily through African National Congress and Pan-African Congress; and International organizations such as the Boycott

Movement, an organization that was founded in London which later metamorphosed into the Anti-Apartheid Movement (AAM) that was at the forefront of lobbying several countries, the Organization of African Union (OAU) through the Mogadishu Declaration of 1971, the Commonwealth through the economic sanctions in 1986, the International Olympics Committee (IOC) that barred the apartheid regime from 1964 Tokyo games and 1968 Mexico games, the United Nations (UN) through various voluntary embargoes such as resolution 1761 and 81.

I have mentioned several individuals, local associations, countries, and international organizations involved in the apartheid struggle, yet one name—Nelson Mandela—appears to resonate most concerning the struggle. Therefore, Nelson Mandela is the root legacy of the apartheid struggle in South Africa; however, Nelson Mandela neither started the struggle nor paid the ultimate price: death. Granted that the apartheid regime imprisoned him for 27 years, but he did not pay the maximum price. Somehow, history positioned him to be the root legacy of the apartheid struggle. It is noteworthy that Nelson Mandela being the root legacy of the apartheid struggle, does not undermine the efforts of several individuals, local associations, countries, and international organizations towards the successful dismantling of the apartheid policy.

2)   *Family legacy*

Some legacies are associated with a family. Often, the last name appears to be more prominent than the other names. Instances are Hitler, in Adolf Hitler of Germany; Mandela, in Nelson Mandela of South Africa; Stalin, in Joseph Stalin of the Soviet Union; Gaddafi, in Muammar Gaddafi of Libya; and Escobar, in Pablo Escobar of the Medellin drug cartel. In some cases, the first name could carry relatively equal weight with the last name: Idi Amin of Uganda and Saddam Hussein of Iraq. If any of one's names is Hitler, Mandela, or Stalin, it brings the memories of what that name symbolizes. Somebody who bears the name will enjoy its goodwill or endure the infamy. I will explore Pablo Escobar's family legacy below for emphasis.

Lessons from Pablo Escobar's family legacy

Pablo Escobar was a Colombian drug baron that strutted the illicit trade between 1976 and 1993 like a colossus. Pablo created several enemies: individuals, rival cartel members, law enforcement agents, journalists, government officials, and politicians; he assassinated a host of them. Following a firefight with the Colombian police force on December 2, 1993, he died of the ensuing gunshot wounds. The nuclear family he left behind include Wife, Maria Victoria Henao Escobar, now goes by the name, Maria Isabel Santos Caballero; son, Juan Pablo Escobar, now goes by the name, Juan Sebastine Marroquin Santos; and daughter, Manuela Escobar, now goes by the name, Juana Manuela Marroquin Santos.

After the death of Pablo Escobar, his wife, Maria, and two children, Juan and Manuela, were forced to take up an entire floor of a hotel in Bogota, Colombia's capital. The Colombian government forces guarded them because the family was at risk of elimination by Pablo's enemies, principally the Cali cartel and *Los Pepes* (an acronym meaning People Persecuted by Pablo Escobar). Aside from protecting the family from harm, the additional motivation to protect them may not be unconnected with the need of the Colombian authorities to trace and confiscate Pablo's enormous assets, mainly United States' Dollars scattered all over Colombia. The country became conspicuously unsafe for Pablo's family forcing them to seek asylum in several countries, but no country was ready to accept them. They went to Mozambique, Brazil, and eventually settled in Argentina on tourist visas with changed identities.

Juan Pablo Escobar is currently into architectural practice and lecturing. He has authored two books around his father's past—*Sins of*

My Father and *Pablo Escobar: My Father*—with his original name, Juan Pablo Escobar. Little is known of Manuela aside from her change of name. I could gather in my quest that she was most adversely affected by the turn of events in her family's fortunes and legacy; she was allegedly deafened in one ear following the Monaco building bombing in 1988. Manuela reportedly went into depression and was accommodated in Argentina by her elder brother, Juan. Maria, Pablo's wife, went into estate management in Argentina. When their identities were made public by a television show, the Argentine authorities detained Juan and Maria for fifteen months on alleged money laundering charges; they later dropped the charges for want of evidence.

Pablo's father, Abel De Jesus Escobar Echeverri, separated from Pablo's mother when Pablo and his siblings were young. Senior Escobar played little or no role in Pablo's lifestyle. He lived most of his life as a hermit working in his livestock and poultry farms. In 1993, the year Pablo died, he visited his father, and Abel purportedly berated Pablo for going into crime. When Pablo was on the run, the Colombian authorities and opposing cartels harassed Abel on many occasions for Pablo's whereabouts. Luz Maria, one of his daughters, asserts that they once kidnapped him in 1985, but the manner of his release is hazy. Abel died in 2001.

Pablo's mother, Hermilda Gaviria de Escobar, had seven children for Pablo's father: Roberto, Pablo, Alba Marina, Luz Maria, Luis Fernando, Argemiro, and Gloria Ines. They divorced while Pablo was still young; Pablo and his siblings were essentially products of single parenting. Hermilda was a devoted mother that loved Pablo to death; however, motherly love appears to have clouded her reasoning. She never believed Pablo was a criminal and blamed virtually everyone except herself and Pablo for his death: the police, the Colombian government, the American government, and journalists. She was never ashamed to be identified with Pablo and often visited his tomb until her death in 2006 at 89 years. The Colombian authorities reportedly found an unmailed letter in Pablo's pocket that he addressed to his mother when he was shot.

Roberto de Jesus Escobar Gaviria is the immediate elder brother of Pablo and the eldest of the siblings; he was a co-founder of the Medellin cartel and the financial controller. He went on the run along with Pablo but turned himself in to the authorities before Pablo was killed, and they imprisoned him. Shortly after Pablo's death, while in prison, his family's past caught up with him through a letter bomb; presumably from one of the rivals that blinded one of his eyes and deafened an ear. The authorities released him in 2006 after over a decade in prison. Roberto has since reinvented himself and is now a technology entrepreneur. He launched a propane touch in 2019 and a foldable phone *Escobar Fold 1'* later the same year. Roberto also incorporated 'Escobar Inc' claiming the sole right to the Pablo Escobar brand. Through his company, Roberto has launched his cryptocurrency, *Dietbitcoin,* and authored a book, *Pablo Escobar's Dietbitcoin.* In the book, he revealed the origin and ownership of cryptocurrencies. Roberto has fought two high-profile cases: he sued Elon Musk for intellectual property theft regarding the *flamethrower,* and another separate case, *Apple,* for $2.6billion in damages over security lapse on the *iPhoneX,* and for misinforming the public about the phone's vulnerability.

Alba Marina is the younger sister of Pablo. She is believed to be one of the closest siblings to Pablo, but there is no account of her involvement in the illicit business. However, Juan claimed that he suspects that she confiscated the two caches of cash stashed away in two separate locations in the *blue house* (one of Pablo's residences) that he revealed to her. Alba Marina authored *El Otro Pablo,* literally meaning, *The Other Pablo,* in Spanish.

Luis Fernando Escobar Gaviria is Pablo's younger brother. He did not get involved in the cartel; instead, he pursued education. In 1977, a drunken police officer, Eliecer, killed him and his girlfriend by forcing them into Luis's car and drove them down a cliff in an apparent murder-suicide act. The rationale for the killing is uncertain, but the connection is that Eliecer was an undercover police officer that once investigated Pablo. The authorities had withdrawn Eliecer from Pablo's assignment because of a lack of progress.

Luz Maria Escobar is another younger sister of Pablo; she claimed that the family knew nothing of Pablo's criminal activities until he told them himself in 1980 that he headed a mafia organization.

Little of Argemiro Escobar and Gloria Ines Escobar, Pablo's other younger siblings, are public. Although a few of their pictures are on the internet, little or nothing of their activities, professional or social lives, and family events are out there. It may not be unconnected with their need to go low profile and stay away from the spotlight, not to resurrect the negative legacy of the family, just as Manuela, Pablo's daughter, may have done.

Juan Carlos Ortiz Escobar is Pablo's nephew; he was one of the high-ranking members of the Cali cartel. There is no record of him working for the Medellin cartel headed by two of his uncles; however, joining the illegal business may not be unconnected with the perceived success of his two uncles. It is noteworthy that he chose to join a rival cartel, and they trusted him enough to get to a prominent position in a group fighting a bitter war with his uncles. Juan later formed the Norte del Valle cartel with some other high-ranking members of the Cali cartel when the Colombian authorities forced the Rodriguez Orejuela brothers to dismantle the Cali cartel and surrender themselves. Wilber Valera, the then head of Norte del Valle cartel, allegedly ordered the murder of Juan Carlos in 2002, shortly after Juan Carlos completed a jail term. The reason for his murder is unclear.

Looking at the lives of Pablo Escobar's family, Pablo's legacy appears to have affected almost every member. Pablo's nuclear family had to relocate to Argentina under false names. In one of Juan's interviews that I watched on YouTube, he claimed that no airline was ready to sell tickets to the family because of their family name, Escobar. He further asserted that the moment they changed their names, they got tickets and could leave Colombia.

3)   Indirect/Associative legacy

Anyone could be associated with a specific legacy without being directly connected to the root legacy. It could occur by bearing either of the names of a root legacy: Muammar, Gaddafi, Amin, Hussein, Saddam, and Stalin. My first name is Ambrose, and I come from a former state in Nigeria, Bendel (Now divided into Delta and Edo states). There was a governor of the then Bendel state (1979–83), the late Ambrose Alli. The general belief is that he ruled Bendel state reasonably well and brought free education to the state at primary and high school levels. When the military took power in 1983 in Nigeria, Ambrose Alli was arrested and tried for corruption in a tribunal. The military found him guilty and sentenced him to 100 years imprisonment for misappropriating N983,000 (Nine hundred and eighty-three thousand Nigerian Naira), about $1.36million as of 1983, meant for a road project. Ambrose Alli told the tribunal that he did not have that amount of money. A Good Samaritan, Chief Gabriel Igbinedion, the Esama (a title in Benin kingdom) of Benin, Nigeria, paid off the government, and the military released him. The corruption charges and conviction did not diminish his legacy as one of the best governors Nigeria has had. Fast forward to 2021, roughly forty years later, when I mention my name in some places, I am still associated with Ambrose Alli. Professor Ambrose Alli did not know me; we do not come from the same local government in Bendel State. Following the division of Bendel state into two, he was from Edo state, while I come from Delta state. My association with him is only our first names.

4)   *City legacy*

Pablo Escobar's and the Cali brothers' drug cartels operated mainly from Medellin and Cali, respectively, Colombia's second and third largest cities. Nonetheless, the United States was the primary market for the drugs they shipped out. The two cartels became famous for the wrong reasons; Medellin and Cali were the headquarters of drug trafficking and violence in Colombia between the mid-eighties and early nineties. While Colombia got tainted with the unpleasant legacy, Medellin and Cali were the city legacies of narco-terrorism in Colombia.

The Medellin cartel appears to eclipse other cartels in violence and popularity. Aside from killing police officers, judges, government officials, and politicians, they were also involved in a war of supremacy with rival groups, notably the Cali cartel and *Los Pepes*. The rival wars increased the number of kidnappings and assassinations, thereby accentuating the notoriety of the two cities involved, Medellin and Cali. The notoriety of Medellin and Cali made Colombia the murder and drug war capital of the world in that period.

Cali is Colombia's third-largest city by landmass and population, Medellin is second, and Bogota is the largest city and capital. Pablo formed the Medellin cartel in 1976, about the same time, Gilberto Rodriguez Orejuela, Miguel Rodriguez Orejuela, Jose Santacruz Londono, and Helmer Herrera Buitrago formed the Cali cartel that was named after the city they lived, Cali. Like Pablo, the Cali cartel started as regular criminals with kidnapping as their primary activity. They received hefty ransoms from foreign nationals they had kidnapped; later, they went into marijuana smuggling. Due to the bulkiness of marijuana and the low-profit margin, they shifted their focus to a more lucrative drug—cocaine. Cali and Medellin cartels shared their target market's cities (The United States). Medellin cartel controlled South Florida and Miami, while Cali cartel controlled New York City; either cartel grabbed other major cities.

At the outset, Cali and Medellin cartels were not at each other's throats; they were more of collaborators. When a guerrilla group, M-19, kidnapped Marta Nieves Ochoa, a sister of the leaders of the Medellin cartel, Ochoa brothers; Medellin and Cali cartels came together to form a group, *MAS* (Muerte e Secuestradores), meaning *Dead to Kidnappers* in Spanish. When MAS captured and tortured M-19 members, they released Marta. The cartels also collaborated in distribution networks and undermined government authority through bribery. Their collaboration allegedly developed cracks when the Medellin cartel made incursions into the New York cocaine market. The arrest of Jorge Ochoa, one of the Medellin cartel leaders, also created suspicion between the two cartels. Helmer Herrera Buitrago, one of the Cali cartel's top leaders, was suspected of having masterminded the bombing of the Pablo-owned Monaco building in 1990. The suspicion led to Helmer's assassination attempt in a football event by Medellin Cartel. Cali cartel purportedly funded *Los PePes*, a group formed by the enemies of Pablo Escobar; their primary goal was to track down and assassinate all associates of the Medellin cartel.

Cali cartel was savvier and more discreet in their illicit business dealings. A clear departure from the brazen manner the Medellin cartel carried out their activities. They preferred to negotiate and bribe government officials instead of intimidation and violence. However, they did not shy away from violence where necessary.

As with any business built on the wrong foundation of illicitness, it is bound to meet its waterloo. By 1996, The Colombian and United States authorities had dismantled Cali cartel's leadership; Rodriguez Orejuela brothers were arrested, imprisoned, and extradited to the United States to face drug charges. Jose Santacruz Londono was arrested and imprisoned in 1995; he later escaped in 1996 but was killed by the police the same year after leaving a shopping mall. The police were tipped-off by an anonymous caller. Helmer Herrera Buitrago turned himself in 1996, but one of his former associates, Rafael Angel Uribe, assassinated him in November 1998 inside the prison while he was playing football. The motive for his killing is unclear, but fingers were pointed at the Norte del Valle cartel.

Norte del Valle cartel is an offshoot of Cali cartel. Following pressure on Rodriguez Orejuela brothers from both Colombian and United States governments, the Cali cartel was forced to negotiate a deal that entailed dismantling their operations for a lighter sentence. They informed all their lieutenants of their decision, but not all of them agreed to toe that line. Orlando Henao Montoya, Juan Carlos Ortiz Escobar, Carlos Alberto Rentería Mantilla, Juan Carlos Ramírez Abadía, and Diego León Montoya Sánchez, all former lieutenants of Cali cartel, formed the Norte del Valle cartel. However, a combination of internal wrangling, gang warfare, arrests, and extraditions decimated the group. As of 2008, the group had become fragmented.

5)   *Tribal legacy*

I view tribal legacy as a combination of idiosyncrasies predominant in people from the same locale, which forms what could be referred to as a culture. When cultural attributes are linked to a tribe, it is safe to call it a tribal legacy. Attributes are termed tribal if their legacies cannot be associated with a specific person or family but a tribe or race.

There is a tribe in Nigeria that has a negative legacy of trading dubiously; even if they give you their best prices, you are wont to feel cheated. Also, another tribe is known for being deliberately deceitful; they resort to lies at the slightest opportunity. When they narrate an incident, you will need to double-check the facts before accepting their story. To ascertain the legacy of a tribe or race, what comes to your mind when you get to know the person's tribe or race? What opinion will you form? What adjustment will you need to make? The consensual answer, or in some cases, answers to the posed questions, is the legacy of that tribe.

6)   Regional legacy

Regions can acquire specific legacies just as one can ascribe a legacy to a city, state, or province. For instance, a region in Italy, Sicily, has a legacy of the mafia. The general belief is that the mafia originated from that region before they exported it to other parts of the world, especially North America. Italy has twenty regions, and five of them are autonomous. Sicily is one of the five autonomous regions; it is also the largest island in the Mediterranean.

Historical background of the mafia

The public generally refers to it as the mafia; however, they call themselves by different names: *Cosa Nostra* (our thing), honorable men, men of respect, and the honored society. Mafia in Italian means swagger; it could also mean boldness or courage. The word mafia has Arabic routes because Sicily was once an Islamic emirate. Variants of the Arabic words include exempted, aggressive boasting, bragging, safety, and protection. The mafia started initially as organizations of largely independent gangs that controlled localities, towns, and cities with similar codes of conduct involved in protection racketeering. They also carried out extra-legal arbitrations following the inability of the government to cater to the increasing need for arbitration over land disputes in Sicily in that period. The land disputes in Sicily grew because of the increase in landowners and security challenges in Sicily in the 19th century. The mafia back then was also used to protect agricultural produce. At some point, they were involved in politics; they bullied voters for their candidates.

Protection racketeering is an unethical security arrangement outside the conventional security setting where equally dangerous organizations offer protection to individuals, politicians, businesses, and institutions against attacks from robbery, looting, piracy, violence, and other hazardous threats posed by other individuals or groups of men of the underworld. The protection comes with a fee or other non-monetary benefits to the mafia offering the service. Usually, it occurs in environments where the state's law enforcement agents do not appear to be in total control of the citizen's security. People and organizations needed the extra layer of security to avoid losses and intimidation.

Protection racketeering is closely related to the modern private security arrangement, but it is slightly different. In a private security arrangement, a client usually sought their services out of his volition: on a need-to-have basis. But in protection racketeering, you will be exposed to a backlash or aggressive behavior from the mafia if you do not seek their services—implying compulsion. It is almost impossible to get out of the arrangement because the mafia control is usually territorial; unlike private security where one can change security providers at will.

Over the years, the mafia has stretched its tentacles beyond protection racketeering, mediation on disagreements between men of the underworld, arrangement, and supervision of illicit agreements and deals. They are also involved in bootlegging, extortion, illegal gambling, prostitution, loan sharking, gambling, labor racketeering, money laundering, infiltration of legitimate businesses, tax fraud schemes, stock manipulation schemes, and drug trafficking.

The organizational structure of a family or clan

A boss or *capofamiglia* heads a clan in a typical mafia clan organizational structure; he is frequently called the Don or Godfather. The boss receives a percentage of every revenue earned by the family. In choosing the boss, the captains vote to select the boss, and the underboss decides where there is a tie. The underboss or *sottocapo* directly aids the boss, and he runs the day-to-day operations of the family rackets. The boss appoints the underboss; he takes over temporarily as the boss if illness, imprisonment, or death incapacitates the boss.

The adviser or *consigliere* serves as an adviser to the boss and reports directly to him. However, he has no reporting line under him in the family. The adviser is usually an appointee of the boss and is usually his most trusted confidante. He is technically the third-ranking member of the family. The adviser also helps to resolve disputes within the family and oversees financial matters. The family views the adviser as an impartial judge with no conflict of interest.

The *caporegime (capo)* or captain heads the armed and operational wing, usually a crew of about ten soldiers; the number of soldiers varies depending on the clan's size. The captain is customarily an appointee of the boss and reports to either the boss or the underboss. The *capo* handles several operations, including rackets, drugs, and murder. The captain heads the business area under his control. *Capos* wield lots of power, especially if he has direct access to the boss.

Soldiers are the core operational staff; they are usually of Sicilian extraction and are seen as untouchable by other families. Other families can only harm a soldier in another family if the soldier's boss approves. The murder of a soldier by another family can spark a war between families; they try to avoid it. Families get their soldiers from a pool of associates that have proven their worth.

The associates are the least on the ladder; family members see them as lackeys they can dispense with at will. They are not viewed as genuine family members but as valuable assets for their operations. Associates include corrupted government officials and prospective Mafioso; the *capo* usually controls them.

The mafia's code of conduct

The mafia is believed to operate with a specific code of conduct referred to as the *Ten Commandments*; the Sicilian police allegedly discovered it from the hideout of a mafia boss, Salvatore Lo Piccolo, in 2007. The purported ten commandments are listed below:

<ol style="list-style-type: upper-roman">
<li>No one can approach another of our friends directly; a third party must do it</li>
<li>Do not befriend the wives of friends</li>
<li>Do not have anything to do with a cop</li>
<li>Do not go to pubs and clubs</li>
<li>You must be available for Cosa Nostra at all times, even when your wife wants to give birth</li>
<li>The family member must respect appointments</li>
<li>We must treat our wives with dignity</li>
<li>Never tell lies to family</li>
<li>You cannot use another family's money</li>
<li>People who cannot be a Cosa Nostra are close relatives in the police department, a two-timer in the family, and anyone with low moral values.</li>
</ol>

Traditionally, only men were Mafiosi, but over the years, there are reports that women have joined the group following the demise or imprisonment of close family members. Women have taken up leadership roles in families to fill up the vacuum created by such circumstances.

The American mafia

Two major factors contributed to the growth of the mafia in the United States; first, the 18th Amendment to the United States Constitution prohibited the manufacture and distribution of alcohol within the United States in 1919. Also, at about the same time, in the early 1920s, the then prime minister of Italy, Benito Mussolini, who ran a Fascist regime, cracked down on the Sicilian Mafia; several of them fled to the United States.

Alcohol prohibition in the United States did not stem the demand for alcohol per se; instead, it created an illegal market. The mafia members in the United States saw the opportunity and joined the lucrative bootlegging business.

The code of Omerta

One of the core characteristics of the mafia is the code of Omerta. It means the code of silence and honor. The characteristics of the code are non-disclosure and non-betrayal of a fellow mafioso even under duress; the penalty for such transgression is usually death that could extend to the transgressor's family members. It also entails non-interference with the activities of other Mafiosi.

A mafioso should not have close ties with law enforcement agents unless for the convenient reason of using the agent as a dispensable associate. Mafiosi should avoid reporting personal losses to the police; instead, they should deal with such matters personally. Dealing with the issue by themself helps to keep their reputation of having the ability to protect others. Mafiosi are expected to be reticent and avoid expressiveness both in disposition and actions. They should eschew drugs and alcohol; it could undermine their self-control.

Mafia and politics

It is not uncommon for politicians to court some mafia bosses to gain political advantage during elections. Mafias control localities and could influence votes in any district they operate. Every man of honor is estimated to have up to 50 protégées. In an area where there are 2,000 men of honor, that could amount to 100,000 votes. A single endorsement from a mafia boss from a locale could generate that many votes; the mafia-endorsed politician would be in a vantage position in that domain. In return for such favors, the politician could assist the mafia boss in undermining police investigations, influence judges, contracts awards, and assistance in getting permits to operate certain businesses: casinos and pubs.

7)   *National legacy*

Countries are usually identified with specific narratives. A country comprises different tribes; each tribe consists of families, and individuals make up a family. I have traced legacy at the individual/root, family, tribal, city, and regional levels. A country is a potpourri of different legacies, but one or a few of these legacies stand out. The legacy is what every other nationality attribute to that country. For instance, Nigerians are believed to have a legacy of being dubious. I watched a video of a young man, Daniel (actual name from Nigeria); he attended a film festival in London and danced with a white girl. The moment he jokingly said he would take her back to Nigeria, the girl exclaimed, "you are from Nigeria!" and ran away from him immediately. That action implied that she did not want to associate with Nigerians. Several countries have built different legacies over the years. Examples include high-quality products: Japan, Germany, and England; Mass production and martial arts: China; and human rights and freedom of expression: the United States. Legacies that are more predominant in a country will be the national legacy of the country.

One can view the source of the national legacy from the perspective of the predominant tribe that interacts more with other countries. In such a case, the dominant legacy of that tribe would likely be the national legacy of that country. For instance, in Nigeria, the Igbos (A tribe from the southeast part of Nigeria) have a penchant for traveling abroad. They are not the majority tribe, but the Igbo's legacy showcased globally is frequently taken as Nigerian legacy. Therefore, a Nigerian abroad is likely going to be associated with the Igbo's legacy.

Nigeria is known for two main negative legacies: Advance Fee Fraud and corruption of public officials. I will focus only on advanced fee fraud here.

Advance Fee Fraud

Advance Fee Fraud is popularly known as 419 in Nigeria; it was coined from chapter 38, section 419 of Nigeria's criminal code bordering on penalties for pretense and cheating. Interestingly, section 419 of the Indian criminal code addresses a similar situation: punishment for cheating by personation. Advance Fee Fraud is the process of obtaining by deception assets, usually money, from gullible, unsuspecting members of the public by faceless criminals. They deceive their victims by making promises they are aware of from the outset that they will not fulfill. The initial cost put forward is usually far less than the promised loot to the victims; the perpetrators would present these costs in the form of processing fees. The fees continue to increase until the victim can no longer pay more money or realizes the deception.

The process usually takes the following structure: first, the criminal will request for assistance or partnership to help access some funds or assets locked up somewhere, usually in a government establishment, from unsuspecting members of the public, and the criminal claim that he cannot access the funds directly without external help. The assets or money, which is purportedly in hundreds of millions of US Dollars, is always too good to turn down. Second, the victim is required to provide a foreign bank account, front as the authentic beneficiary of the transaction, and fund the facilitation fee. The facilitation fee is initially presented to the victim as a small fraction of the expected loot and is often affordable—it is a bait. As soon as the victim pays the initial fee, the criminals will create another layer of hurdle that will require parting with some money to overcome. Each challenge comes with an additional fee; this will continue until the victim can no longer afford to pay more money or realizes that he is being scammed. The perpetrators pretend to handle all the transactions until the victim's account is credited. The criminal and the victim are supposed to share the proceeds of the loot under an agreed sharing formula. The reality is that there is no money or asset anywhere.

Advance Fee Fraud did not originate from Nigeria. Historical records show that variants of such schemes have existed as far back as the 18th century in Spain, 19th century in Jerusalem, and 20th century in Germany. In Nigeria, the scam became popular in the late nineteen eighties and has not abated since then. Young and usually unemployed Nigerians started printing and posting letters to prospective victims through the mailing system using foreign yellow pages to get foreign addresses. The advent of the internet has facilitated the move of the illicit business into the digital space. During the early stages of the digital revolution in Nigeria, several cybercafés were spread across the country; the cybercafés became the offices for the criminals. The emergence of portable modems and smartphones have further moved their operations to remote locations.

The scams usually come in various forms:
i)   Assistance/partnership to assist in recovering looted funds holed up somewhere or a contract already awarded and budgeted. The criminal will need a front to present as the authentic beneficiary of the fund.
ii) Romance scams where the criminals prey on their victim's emotions to get their confidence and emotional involvement, then tweak them to any of their schemes. It could include asking them to come to their country of operation; the criminals usually change their behavior and become aggressive after the victim's arrival. It could consist of kidnapping and sometimes, murder; this method has been reported in several countries.
iii) Other scams are bogus lottery wins; non-existent job offers in blue-chip companies with a mouth-watering package, but the victim will bear the relocation costs; online sales and rentals through fake check overpayment; and pet scams through asking for transportation fees.

Ironically, Nigeria is publicized globally as a nation whose citizens drive advance fee fraud and other fraudulent schemes. Research done in 2006 shows that only 6% of scams originated from Nigeria; the United States and the United Kingdom account for 61% and 16% respectively. Nevertheless, the report only stated the countries where the scams originated but did not include the perpetrators' nationalities.

Recently, in Nigeria, a new set of internet scammers have sprung up; they are called *yahoo yahoo*. The group appears to be more brazen and is involved in the identity theft of individuals, organizations, and governments. Their process involves compromising people's data and using it to transact businesses online. It also includes transaction diversion through personation; the United States government lost millions of US Dollars to scammers through personation during the COVID-19 relief payout.

8)   Continental legacy

Continental legacy is like a funnel; the legacies of individual countries in the continent compete for attention. The national legacy of the most predominant country appears to showcase at the continental level. However, several people from other continents appear to separate different countries and their legacies. In the American continent, North and South America, the United States has a legacy for business and a land of opportunities. Argentina, another country in America, has a legacy for football, and Brazil, football.

Legacies are often ascribed to countries, but they can sometimes be associated with certain continents on a blanket level. For example, the world views Africa as a continent (of corrupt leaders, where they are not held accountable) fraught with poverty, insecurity, and underdevelopment. While many countries in Africa could be associated with such negative legacies, not all countries are in that bracket.

The world now associates the Middle East transcontinental region with wealth because several Arab nations have accumulated wealth from oil export. It is noteworthy that not all Arab nations are wealthy. The United Arab Emirates, Kuwait, Qatar, and Saudi Arabia are the wealthy countries in the Middle East; they have swayed the world's opinion to view the Middle East countries as wealthy. The wealth of the leading Arab nations has overshadowed the struggling nations: Lebanon, Afghanistan, and Yemen.

Just like national legacy, the country that interacts more with the other continents normally showcases its legacies. However, government agencies and news agencies of other countries in different continents appear to be more knowledgeable about individual countries' uniqueness. Consequently, they are better positioned to appreciate the legacies of individual countries rather than using a blanket classification.

3 ACCIDENTAL LEGACY

"Slightest accidents open up new worlds."

......Jeanette Winterson

Some persons and events shaped our world; they left lasting legacies, but the persons involved were not willing participants in making the events. However, providence placed them to be at the center. I will explore two instances where three actors were directly involved, nonetheless, accidentally: Archduke Franz Ferdinand—World War 1 and Trayvon Martin and George Floyd—Black Lives Matter movement. Although many others were also involved in making these events, they were not as prominent as the earlier mentioned actors.

Archduke Franz Ferdinand (1863–1914) and World War 1

Archduke Franz Ferdinand was born in the Austria-Hungary Empire's royal family, but he was not in the direct line of the throne. His first cousin, Crown Prince Rudolf Karl Joseph (1858–1889), was the heir apparent. Rudolf's father, Franz Joseph, was Austria–Hungary's emperor.

Crown Prince Rudolf Karl Joseph was the only son of Emperor Franz Joseph and Empress Elizabeth. He developed an interest in natural sciences when he was young and became an avid collector of minerals; Vienna University of agriculture inherited most of them after his death. His marriage to Princess Stephanie of Belgium in 1881 was initially blissful, but it later developed cracks that led to him finding solace in drinking and other female companions. The Crown Prince muted the idea of annulling the marriage; his father, the emperor, rebuffed it. His flirtations with other female companions exposed the couple to contracting gonorrhea, which rendered Princess Stephanie sterile.

In late 1888, the Crown Prince fell in love with 17-year-old Marie Frein Von Vetsera. In 1886, Crown Prince Rudolf had bought a hunting lodge, Mayerling. On January 30, 1889, Crown Prince Rudolf and young Marie Frein Von Vetsera were found dead in Mayerling lodge in an apparent joint suicide. The secret letter found in 2015 that was kept in a safe deposit box in a bank by Marie where she stated the plan to commit suicide with Crown Prince Rudolf confirmed the incident in Mayerling lodge of 1889. The motive for the action is unclear, but the official position of the empire is a mental imbalance of the Crown Prince. The act of the Crown Prince caused much pain to his parents, especially his mother, Empress Elizabeth. Throughout her lifetime, she mourned her son's death by continuously wearing mourning clothes and living most of her life outside the imperial court in Vienna until Luigi Lucheni, an Italian anarchist, murdered her in Geneva, Switzerland, in 1898.

World War I, which caused the entire world an unprecedented carnage, had an indirect link to the suicide of Crown Prince Joseph. I will explore how these actions connect later in this chapter.

Since Emperor Franz Joseph had no other son, his younger brother, Archduke Karl Ludwig, the father of Archduke Franz Ferdinand, became the next in line. Unfortunately, Archduke Karl Ludwig died of typhoid fever shortly after returning from Palestine and Egypt in 1896 while Emperor Franz Joseph was still on the throne. The death of Archduke Karl Ludwig made his first son, Archduke Franz Ferdinand, the heir presumptive. It is termed heir presumptive because if Emperor Franz Joseph happened to have had a son before he died, the son would have become the heir apparent.

Archduke Franz Ferdinand was interested in trophy hunting and travels. Despite his official responsibilities and possible busy schedule, between 1892 and 1893, he found time to circumnavigate the world. His interest in trophy hunting resulted in the death of over 270,000 animals he directly killed; the sport enthralled the Archduke so much that he kept a personal diary of all the animals he had killed.

In 1894, Archduke Ferdinand fell in love with Sophie Chotek and they wanted to get married, but there was an obstacle. Although Sophie was of a noble class, she was not a descendant of any ruling family—a condition precedent for them to marry. The kingmakers left Archduke Franz Ferdinand with two tough choices: abandon the proposed marriage or carry out a morganatic marriage; Archduke Franz Ferdinand chose the latter. Morganatic marriage has several implications: none of their offspring will be eligible to ascend the throne of Austria-Hungary Empire, the ruling class will not accept Sophie, she cannot bear her husband's ranks, will not ride with her husband in the royal carriage, will not appear with the Archduke in any official function, and they cannot share the royal box in the theater together. What a price to pay for love! Archduke Franz Ferdinand and Sophie married in 1900 despite the stringent conditions.

On June 28, 1914, during an official visit to Bosnia and Herzegovina, a province of the Austria-Hungary Empire, Archduke Franz Ferdinand was murdered along with his wife, Sophie, in Sarajevo, the provincial capital, by Gavrilo Princip, a 17-year-old member of *Young Bosnia*. The murder of the couple was uncanny because they had earlier survived an assassination attempt by the same group in the morning, on the streets of Sarajevo, when a member of *Young Bosnia*, Nedeljko Cabrinovic, threw a grenade at their car. The grenade bounced off the car's back and exploded under the vehicle behind them in the motorcade; the explosive injured the occupants.

Shortly after getting to the governor's residence and taking some rest, Archduke Franz Ferdinand insisted that he wanted to see how the injured members of his entourage were faring in the hospital. He got into the car with his wife, Sophie, and they went back to the streets of Sarajevo. Unknown to the Chauffer, Leopold Lojka, the itinerary had changed, and he made a wrong turn. In an attempt to reverse the vehicle, it stalled. Opposite where the car stalled was Gavrilo Princip, one of the assassins that might have accepted that they had failed in their bid to murder the Archduke. Gavrilo walked across to the car and fired two shots at close range with a pistol. One bullet hit Sophie in the stomach, and the other hit Archduke Franz Ferdinand in the neck. Sophie died on their way to the hospital, while the Archduke died shortly after arriving in the hospital.

Young Bosnia is a revolutionary movement comprising young students of Serbian origin with Croats and Muslims. Its primary objectives centered on the unification of Yugoslavian and Serbian territories. Ironically, the *Young Bosnia* is a product of Austria-Hungary's policy to improve infrastructure and education in their newly gained Bosnia territory. The policy thrust created the avenue to foster the revolutionary movement that undermined Austria-Hungary objectives in Bosnia. The *Black Hand* is a secret organization rooted in the Serbian military; they trained and armed the *Young Bosnia*.

It was alleged that the *Black Hand* decided to murder Archduke Ferdinand because they saw him as having a reconciliatory disposition towards Serbia; this position, by their calculation, could undermine their plan for the Serbian revolution. *Young Bosnia's* strategy has been to murder members of the ruling class; Archduke Franz Ferdinand falls into the group. Whether it was the *Black Hand* that ordered the killing of Archduke Franz Ferdinand or the *Young Bosnia*, the fact remains that both organizations were complicit in the murder. The former supplied the training, logistics, and equipment, while the latter had willing personnel.

After the fatal shooting of Archduke Ferdinand and his wife Sophie, Gavrilo Princip attempted to commit suicide by shooting himself, but Archduke's security details quickly overpowered him. During the trial, Gavrilo claimed that he had no intention of shooting Sophie; instead, he had targeted General Oskar Potiorek, the governor of Bosnia and Herzegovina, a passenger in the car that conveyed the Archduke and his wife. Austro-Hungarian authorities tried Gavrilo and his accomplices; they found Gavrilo guilty and sentenced him to 20 years imprisonment, the maximum he could get under the extant Habsburg law. The prison authorities placed Gavrilo in solitary confinement, and he suffered severe conditions—malnutrition and tuberculosis. Tuberculosis weakened his bones so much that his right arm had to be amputated. Gavrilo died on April 28, 1918, weighing barely 40 kilograms, two months short of four years after the assassination incident.

The assassination of Archduke Ferdinand and his wife Sophie set off a series of events that almost consumed the world—World War I. Although the Serbia government was not directly involved in the Archduke's assassination, the involvement of the *Black Hand*, a secret organization with roots in the Serbian military, strained the relationship between Austria-Hungary Empire and Serbia. In anticipation of war, on July 23, 1914, Austria-Hungarian Empire issued a 10-point ultimatum to Serbia that was almost impossible to accept:

1) Smother publications that will prompt scorn and disdain of the Monarchy (Referring to Austria-Hungarian Empire) and the overall propensity, which will be coordinated against the regional honesty of the last-mentioned

2) To continue on the double to the disintegration of the Narodna Odbrana, to seize the entirety of its methods for promulgation, and similarly, to continue against different associations and relationships in Serbia, which possess themselves with purposeful publicity against Austria-Hungary; the Royal Government will accept such measures as are essential to ensure that they broke up affiliations, may not proceed with their exercises under different names or in other structures

3) Dispose of immediately from public guidance in Serbia, everything, regardless of whether associated with the showing corps or with the techniques for educating that serves or may serve to feed the promulgation against Austria-Hungary

4) To remove from the military all officials and supporting structures carrying on the publicity against Austria-Hungary, and whose names the Imperial and Royal Government claims all authority to spread the word about the Royal Government

5) Consent to support in Serbia the organs of the Imperial and Royal Government in the camouflage of defiant advancement, composed against the genuineness of the Monarchy

6) To conduct a judicial investigation into every participant in the June 28 conspiracy who may be found on Serbian territory; the organs of the Imperial and Royal Government representative will take part in the activities

7) Agree to arrest Major Voislav Tankosic and Milan Ciganovitch, Serbian officials, who were alleged to have been compromised following the inquest

8) To stop the participation of Serbian officials in the smuggling of military equipment across its borders; to relieve officers from the

borders post of Schabats and Losnitza that were involved in the Sarajevo crime

9) To justify the Imperial and Royal Government comments concerning the unwarranted utterances of high-ranking Serbian officials in and outside of Serbia; who continually made uncomplimentary remarks towards Austria-Hungary since the assassination of June 28

10) To quickly communicate to the Imperial and Royal Government the update on the execution points above.

The Serbian government accepted all except point six; in their thinking, accepting it would amount to losing their sovereignty. On July 28, 1914, Austria-Hungary, backed by Germany, declared war on Serbia. Between August 1-4, Germany declared war on Russia, France, and Belgium. The declaration of war on Belgium was because of the refusal of Belgium to agree to Germany's request to allow Germany to pass through their territory to attack France. Britain, which had earlier assured France of its support, declared war on Germany on August 4, 1914. Thus, the world became embroiled in a protracted war that ended on November 18, 1918, with an armistice initiated by Germany.

Aided by hindsight, World War I may not have started, or at least, it would have happened much later if some events that caused the war had happened differently. First, the suicide of Crown Prince Rudolf brought Archduke Franz Ferdinand into the picture, and Crown Prince Rudolf may never have gone to Bosnia Herzegovina to inspect the army. Second, going by the reported reason the *Black Hand* ordered the assassination of Archduke Franz Ferdinand: he had a reconciliatory disposition towards Serbia—a position the *Black Hand* thought could undermine the Serbian revolution. Crown Prince Rudolf may not have had the same disposition as Archduke Franz Ferdinand, implying that the *Black Hand* may not have ordered Crown Prince Rudolf's assassination. Therefore, it is not out of place to suggest that the suicide of Crown Prince Rudolf has an indirect connection with World

War I.

Another incidence that may have averted the war was when Archduke Franz Ferdinand visited England in November 1913. He was a guest of the Duke of Portland, Welbeck Abbey, Nottinghamshire, England, and they went game shooting. The loader of the gun fell, and two barrels of the weapon discharged: it missed Archduke Franz Ferdinand and his host by a whisker. The thinking is that suppose the Archduke had died through that accident or was wounded; the assassination would not have happened when it did. It implies that the war might not have had a trigger.

When they reminded Gavrilo of how his action contributed to World War 1, in his response, he averred that even if he did not murder the Archduke, the war would still have occurred. While his position may be plausible, it is still a matter of conjecture as there must be a trigger for a war to start. Nevertheless, it is safe to say that Archduke Franz Ferdinand is the root legacy of World War I, although, accidental. No deliberate action of his caused the war. He did not lobby to become the heir presumptive; providence placed him on that path. Even after he had escaped the first assassination attempt, within a few hours, he found himself on the streets of Sarajevo again when it was apparent that Sarajevo authorities had not eliminated the imminent threat. As they journeyed down the road, General Oskar Potiorek, forgot to inform the chauffeur, Leopold Lojka, about the route change, and he made a wrong turn; that gave Gavrilo the opportunity to murder the heir apparent and his wife. The coincidences are so aligned that I am tempted to believe that this incident had an agreed date with destiny.

Trayvon Martin (1995–2012), George Floyd (1973–2020), and the Black Lives Matter movement

Trayvon Martin was a 17-year-old African American from Miami, Florida, United States. He attended Dr. Michael M. Krop High school in Miami. Trayvon was initially interested in football but later developed an interest in aviation. In pursuit of his aviation dreams, he attended a program in 2009 tagged *Experience Aviation*, a seven-week program organized by Barrington Irving, a famous aviator. According to his parents, Trayvon had plans to attend either the University of Miami or Florida A&M University.

Trayvon was active in social media; he posted several tweets and YouTube videos during his lifetime. In his YouTube videos, Trayvon posted excerpts from the movies he had watched; his enthusiasm for rap music was also evident in his tweets.

Trayvon's parents, Sybrina Fulton and Tracy Martin, divorced when he was four years old. On February 19, 2012, Trayvon visited his father's fiancée, Brandy Green, along with his father, Tracy, in Twin Lake, Sanford, Florida. Krop High School had suspended Trayvon for having traces of drugs in his backpack. Tracy brought Trayvon to Twin Lake to get away from friends and clear his head. After spending a week in Twin Lake, on Sunday evening, February 26, 2012, Trayvon, wearing a hoodie, went to 7-Eleven store to buy some consumables.

On his way back, a resident and neighborhood watch volunteer, George Zimmerman, who is of German and Peruvian ancestry, spotted Trayvon and called 911; he reported the presence of a suspicious guy in the neighborhood. In Zimmerman's words, *"this guy looks like he is up to no good, or he is on drugs or something. It is raining, and he is just walking around."* The dispatcher asked Zimmerman not to bother following the suspicious guy. Although from all indications, Zimmerman did not comply with the dispatcher's directive; there was contact between him and Trayvon after the call to the dispatcher. An altercation ensued between Trayvon and Zimmerman; he shot Trayvon in the chest in self-defense by Zimmerman's admission. According to him, a brief, hot exchange resulted in a scuffle, and Trayvon wrestled Zimmerman to the ground, hitting him severally. The encounter left Zimmermann with a bloodied nose and injuries in his head and temple. He claimed that while Trayvon was on top of him, he called out for help, but none came until he used the gun. Multiple pieces of evidence appear to corroborate Zimmerman's claim. The police met Trayvon lying face down on the grass; efforts by everyone at the scene to revive him were unsuccessful, and he was pronounced dead at 7:30 pm. The police did not charge George Zimmerman for the murder of Trayvon Martin immediately because he claimed to have shot Trayvon in self-defense based on an extant law, *Stand Your Ground*, in Florida. The Stand Your Ground law allows anyone whose life is in danger to use maximum force, including killing, if necessary, to defend and ward off the threat.

The uproar, widespread protests across the United States, media coverage, and petitions forced Florida authorities to charge Zimmerman for murder on April 11, 2012, and a trial followed. The trial was widely debated globally, especially in the United States, where gun culture and racial profiling issues came to the front burner.

On July 13, 2013, the jury acquitted George Zimmerman of second-degree murder and manslaughter charges. The department of justice still investigated Zimmerman for possible culpability of Trayvon's human rights violation; the investigation ended in February 2015 with no concrete evidence.

The acquittal of George Zimmerman had a severe emotional impact on Alicia Garza, an activist, who realized how lowly Black Lives Mattered in the United States. Patrisse Khan-Cullors and Opal (Ayo) Tometi helped her to create the hashtag *#BlackLivesMatter* on various social media platforms. The core objectives of the movement are to fight racism and violence against black people, especially police brutality.

Closely associated with the social media hashtag is the Black Lives Matter Global Network foundation. Activists usually lead a decentralized grassroots movement in local chapters. Although the local groups are somewhat autonomous, the Global Network foundation expects them to operate within their ideals. Black lives Matter Global Network foundation is active in the United States, Canada, and Britain.

Between 2013 and 2020, several killings of African Americans by the police have happened. The Black Lives Matters movement has been directly involved in protests and raising awareness of police brutality.

On October 20, 2014, in Chicago, Illinois, Laquan McDonald was fatally shot by a police officer, Jasen Van Dyke, for brandishing a knife and behaving erratically—the claim was false. Officer Jasen Van Dyke was charged with first-degree murder but was found guilty of second-degree murder and 16 counts of aggravated battery with a firearm.

On November 13, 2014, in Cleveland, Ohio, 12-year-old Tamir Rice was fatally shot by officer Timothy Loehmann following a reported case of a juvenile wielding a gun—the gun was fake. The two officers involved, Timothy Loehmann and Frank Garmback, were not charged following a grand jury review of the case. The police department later fired Timothy Loehmann for providing false information on his job application. The lawsuit instituted by the Rice family against the two officers and the city of Cleveland ended with a settlement of $6m in favor of Rice's family.

On April 4, 2015, in South Carolina, Officer Michael Slager fatally shot Walter Scott while attempting to flee arrest for a non-functioning brake light that later snowballed into a struggle with the police. Michael Slager pleaded guilty to civil rights violations; he was sentenced to 20 years imprisonment for second-degree murder.

On April 19, 2015, Freddie Gray died following injuries he sustained a week earlier on his spinal cord, close to his neck, when arrested and transported by the police for possessing a knife. The six officers involved in his arrest and the driver were indicted and charged for offenses ranging from second-degree murder, involuntary manslaughter, second-degree assault, and false imprisonment. They dropped the cases against officers William G. Porter, Garret E. Miller, Edward M. Nero, and Sgt. Alicia D. White. Officers Ceaser Godison Jr. and Lt. Brian W. Rice were found not guilty.

On July 13, 2015, 28-year-old Sandra Bland was found hanging in her police cell, in Waller County, Texas, following an arrest for a minor traffic offense by Officer Brian Encinia. The police claimed that it was suicide; the grand jury did not see any reason to indict the County Sheriff and the jail staff for any culpability in the death of Sandra. However, FBI and Texas authorities concluded that the Waller County jail did not follow due protocol in handling inmates. They charged Officer Brian Encinia for perjury—making a false statement regarding the incident leading to the arrest of Sandra. Following an agreement with Brian to end his career in law enforcement, they dropped the case.

On July 5, 2016, Alton Sterling was fatally shot by officer Blane Salamoni in Baton Rouge, Louisiana, while he and a fellow officer, Howie Lake, were trying to restrain Sterling that was resisting arrest. The police claimed that Sterling struggled with them and attempted to reach a loaded handgun in his pants pocket, which prompted the shooting. The unfortunate incident occurred following police response to a call of a reported case of a compact disc (CD) seller threatening a man with a gun. An eyewitness said that it was not Sterling that was making the trouble; Sterling had been carrying the gun days earlier in response to robbery attacks on CD sellers.

On July 6, 2016, Philando Castile was fatally shot in his car, in Falcon Heights, Minnesota, by police officer Jeronimo Yanez in the presence of his girlfriend, Diamond Reynolds, and her 4 years old daughter. Officer Yanez thought Castile was attempting to pull out a gun; meanwhile, Castile was only trying to bring out the documents the officer requested. Minnesota authorities charged officer Yanez with second-degree manslaughter and two counts of dangerous discharge of firearms. He was acquitted of both charges: a verdict that did not go down well with public expectation.

On March 13, 2020, in Louisville, Kentucky, a 26-year-old African American young lady, Breonna Taylor, an emergency room technician, was shot at least five times by the police after breaking into her apartment in the middle of the night in a poorly planned and executed attempt to bust a drug ring. The police had earlier received approval for a *no-knock* entry, but they changed it to *knock and announce* shortly before the raid. It is debatable whether the police announced their entry before breaking into Breonna's apartment. The death of Breonna led to a total ban on no-knock search warrants in the Louisville city council and the enactment of Breonna's law, which requires officers to wear body cameras at least five minutes before and after the execution of a search warrant. The estate of Breonna Taylor filed a lawsuit against the officers involved in the incident and the city of Louisville for wrongful death. The Louisville city officials agreed to a $12million settlement in favor of the estate of Breonna Taylor. Brett Hankison and Myles Cosgrove, two of the officers involved, were relieved of their duties, while a third officer, Jonathan Mattingly, was reassigned to another department. The officers claimed to have fired into Breonna's apartment in response to a shot by Kenneth Walker, Breonna's boyfriend. Cosgrove's shots likely killed Breonna.

George Floyd was a 46year old African American with a checkered past; he grew up in Houston, Texas. George played football and basketball in high school and college. He was a hip-hop rapper and part of two music groups: *screwed up click* and *presidential playas*. George attended A&M University, Kingsville, briefly but dropped out in 1995. He was convicted of several crimes between 1997 to 2007; the last was a 5year jail term for robbery.

George was released on parole in 2013 and tried to clean up his acts. He became involved with a Christian ministry, Resurrection Houston, where he mentored young people, engaged in anti-violence advocacy, and meal delivery to the elderly. George moved to Minneapolis in 2014. In search of a saner life, he completed a 90-day rehabilitation program, *Turning Point*, in Minneapolis. George took up a security job and attempted to get a commercial license to operate trucks; he could not complete the program because of the pressure to earn a living. Until his death in May 2020, George continued to struggle with drug addiction.

Interestingly, in 2019, George worked in a nightclub, El Nuevo club, where Officer Derek Chauvin, the police officer that suffocated him, also worked as off-duty security personnel. However, it does not appear they knew each other because of their different work schedules.

In 2020, George worked as a part-time security guard in a nightclub and doubled as a delivery driver. A minor road traffic accident led to discovering that George did not have a commercial driver's license: he gave up the job. George was out of work when the Covid-19 pandemic that paralyzed global economic activities in 2020 struck. He contracted the virus in April the same year but recovered almost immediately.

On May 25, 2020, after buying cigarettes in a grocery store in the Powderhorn neighborhood in Minneapolis, Minnesota, United States, George was accosted by four Minneapolis police officers for allegedly purchasing the cigarettes with a counterfeit 20 Dollar note. Based on the video evidence, he did not resist arrest, yet the police handcuffed and laid him face down on the ground, and one of the officers, Derek Chauvin, knelt on his neck for 9 minutes 29 seconds despite his continuous plea to them that he could not breathe. The other two officers, Thomas Lane and Alexander J. Kueng, assisted Derek in restraining him while the fourth officer, Tou Thao, prevented eyewitnesses from intervening. The eyewitnesses were limited to verbal intervention and recording videos. When the emergency medical technicians arrived, George had become unresponsive for over 2 minutes; it means that he died before their arrival. The Hennepin County medical examiner reported that George died while being restrained by the police, and he declared his death a homicide. He stated several possible causes of his death: cardiopulmonary arrest, complicating law enforcement subdual restraint, and neck compression. The medical examiner further noted that George had other complications that may have contributed to his death: fentanyl intoxication, recent use of methamphetamine, arteriosclerotic heart disease, and hypertensive heart disease.

George Floyd's family was not satisfied with the Hennepin County medical report; they ordered an independent autopsy. Dr. Allexia Wilson and Dr. Michael Baden conducted the autopsy. The autopsy report stated that the death of George was a homicide caused by asphyxia because of the compression on the back and neck.

The death of George caused outrage globally; there were protests all over the United States and around the world. The Black Lives Matter movement returned and took an international dimension. Despite the lockdown following the COVID-19 pandemic, protesters still came out to the streets in large numbers. Initially, the protests were peaceful, but they soon got out of control; looting of shops became rampant in the United States. The Black Lives Matter movement symbol is taking a *kneeling bow*; some sports associations still observe it as of 2021.

The police department immediately fired the officers involved. Minnesota authorities initially charged Derek Chauvin for third-degree murder and second-degree manslaughter. At the same time, they also indicted the other three officers for aiding and abetting third-degree murder and second-degree manslaughter. Each state's laws in the United States define and categorize murder and manslaughter. The state of Minnesota statutes defined third-degree murder as *"The unintentional killing of another through an eminently dangerous act committed with a depraved mind and without regard for human life."* It carries a penalty of up to 25 years imprisonment and or a fine of up to $40,000. Following a global outcry, the authorities upgraded the charges from third-degree murder and second-degree manslaughter to second-degree murder and second-degree manslaughter. Second-degree murder is defined as *"Killing a human intentionally, but without premeditation (not thinking about or preparing for before)' or 'causes the death of a human being without intent to effect the death of any person, while intentionally inflicting or attempting to inflict bodily harm upon the victim, when the perpetrator is restrained under an order for protection, and a victim is a person designated to receive protection under the order."* There are other definitions of second-degree murder in Minnesota statutes; however, the two definitions stated above appear more relevant to this case. Second-degree murder carries a penalty of not more than 40 years; there is no option of a fine in the statute. Second-degree manslaughter is defined as *"death caused by the person's culpable negligence whereby the person creates an unreasonable risk and consciously takes chances of causing death or great bodily harm to another."* Second-degree manslaughter carries a penalty of up to 10 years imprisonment and/or a fine of up to $20,000. Accordingly, the other three officers' charges were upgraded to aiding and abetting second-degree murder and manslaughter. Aiding and abetting is defined as *"a person is criminally liable for a crime committed by another if the person intentionally aids, advises, hires, counsels, or conspires with or otherwise procures the other to commit the crime."* The penalty appears to carry the same weight as the person who carried out the crime. The state of Minnesota agreed to pay the family of George Floyd $27million.

Gorge's brother, Philonise Floyd, created a GoFundMe account to cover burial expenses, logistics, grief counseling, and legal costs. Four days after setting up the fund, it had generated more than $7million and over $13million by June 2020. A second GoFundMe account was created by George's sister, Bridgett Floyd, to raise $5,000 to cover logistics costs, and she deactivated it after raising over $370,000 in a short period.

The killing of George Floyd has brought several challenges to Derek Chauvin. The Minnesota police department fired him. To get a conditional bail in October 2020, he posted a $1million bond; Derek is currently one of the hated men in the world. Derek's ex-wife, Kellie, filed for divorce a few days after his charge for George Floyd's murder. There was a renewed spotlight on his financial dealings; the Minnesota authorities have charged him for tax evasion. The barely 9 minutes act of indiscretion has disrupted his life. Following his conviction on April 20, 2021, they revoked his bail on the three counts of second-degree unintentional murder, third-degree murder, and second-degree manslaughter. The jury sentenced Derek to twenty-two and a half years imprisonment on June 25, 2021.

The three people involved in the two situations under review: Archduke Franz Ferdinand, Trayvon Martin, and George Floyd, were unaware that they would become root legacies of significant world events. They did not willingly play any part in the legacies they are directly associated with aside from being in the wrong place at the wrong time. If the death can perceive, Archduke Franz Ferdinand would be wondering how a routine state visit could end up causing a world war that accounted for the death of estimated 20 million people (10 million combatant soldiers and 10 million civilians). Trayvon Martin would be amazed at how going to buy skittles in a nearby shop, and George Floyd, buying cigarettes around the corner, caused the creation and re-energized such a humongous movement, Black Lives Matter, whose effect reverberates around the world. The involuntariness characterizes what I describe as *accidental legacy*.

4 SUBCONSCIOUS LEGACY

"Train your subconscious to be positive

by using the heart intelligence."

…..Steven Redhead

Some people's efforts could unintentionally create legacies. It differs from accidental legacies where there is no sustained involvement of the root legacy in creating the legacy. Yet, events outside their control make them the center of the event. In subconscious legacy, the root legacy has an active and sustained involvement in the making of the event but is unaware of the ensuing legacy. There is no deliberate attempt by the root legacy to create a legacy from the outset. This legacy is a product of an effort one believes and is actively involved; it could be in one's profession, hobby, or research. It is great if the ensuing legacy is positive; however, it would be embarrassing to produce a negative legacy from this kind of endeavor.

The realization that one's action might inadvertently create a legacy brings to the fore the need for everyone to develop a positive legacy consciousness. It would help develop the ability to assess the future implications of one's current actions.

Subconscious legacy is often posthumous, but sometimes, the root legacy could realize the legacy in their lifetime. I will review the legacies of two persons that would capture this variant of legacy: Edmund Mcllhenny of the Tabasco Sauce and Alfred Nobel, the inventor of the dynamite. Edmund Mcllhenny's legacy was posthumous, while Alfred Nobel's legacy regarding dynamite came to the fore during his lifetime.

Edmund Mcllhenny (1815–1890)

Edmund Mcllhenny is an American-born entrepreneur of Irish and Scottish descent; he started as a banker in Louisiana and later formed his bank. The American civil war, which began in 1861, forced Mcllhenny to flee with his in-laws to Texas, where he worked with the confederate army as a civilian employee. The defeat of the confederate army in 1865 led to the collapse of America's Southern states' economy; it did not spare Mcllhenny's bank. He moved in with his in-laws to Avery Island, Louisiana, and started working in their garden, where he grew fruits and vegetables.

His friend, Maunsel White, a plantation owner, gave him Tabasco pepper and a recipe for Tabasco Pepper Sauce. It is not publicly known whether the first recipe he commercialized in 1868 is the original recipe that White gave to him or its variant. In 1870, he patented the recipe and packaged it in a cologne-type bottle with a sprinkler head; the sauce is best served sprinkled, not poured. Edmund had only one recipe on offer at the outset, and his sales were mainly in New Orleans; he later expanded to New Iberia, Texas, New York, Philadelphia, and Boston. During his lifetime, he produced 350,000 bottles of the sauce.

At his death in 1890, the Tabasco Sauce, although still in production, was not regarded as anything of significance. He neither mentioned it in his autobiography sketch nor was it recognized during his obituary. His sons, John Avery and Edward Avery Mcllhenny realized that their father had left behind a legacy worth sustaining and developing. They embarked on the expansion of the farms and improved the production process. As of 2021, Tabasco Pepper Sauce has grown into a large family business offering eight variants. They currently produce an average of 150,000 bottles per day and sell in over 195 countries worldwide. Tabasco sauce is commonly found as part of military rations and used as additional flavors in restaurants. As with private companies, the financials are not public, but they should be good.

Tabasco Pepper Sauce is one of the few companies in the United States that have survived over one and half centuries with its original identity intact; the Tabasco brand is still a family-owned business. The company typically appoints its chief operating officer (CEO) from a descendant of Edmund Mcllhenny. As of 2021, Harold Osborn, one of the great-grandsons of Edmund Mcllhenny is the CEO of tabasco sauce.

The motivation to develop and market the recipe by Edmund Mcllhenny is hazy. Perhaps, he just wanted to eke out a living, or he wanted to expose the world to the product's unique flavor. However, one can decipher from his actions that he had the know-how to turn an opportunity into a commercial success. Recall that both the Tabasco pepper and the recipe did not come initially from him; Maunsel White, who should have patented and commercialized it, gave it to him. If Mcllhenny had the ambition of creating a legacy out of the sauce, he may have given up or did not see it in that light since he did not directly pass on any plan to his children. It took the foresight and innovativeness of John and Edward to harness the recipe's intrinsic value, which accentuated the earlier work of their father, Edmund.

Alfred Nobel (1833–1896)

Alfred Nobel was a Swedish scientist, engineer, inventor, and businessman. Alfred's father, Immanuel Nobel (1801–1872), was a civil engineer and inventor; he specialized in building bridges and roads. Immanuel aroused his children's interest in business and inventions.

Immanuel Nobel had several business failures in Sweden. As a result, he moved to Saint Petersburg, Russia, where he became a successful military equipment manufacturer for the Russian Army during the Crimean war. Immanuel invented the Rotary Lathe machine used in woodwork; he also invented nitroglycerin, a volatile explosive. When the Crimean war ended in 1856, the demand for military equipment tapered; consequently, Immanuel Nobel's company faced bankruptcy: he returned to Sweden.

Alfred Nobel left Russia for Paris in 1850 to study chemistry. He later moved to the United States to work under the supervision of John Ericsson to continue his training. Alfred moved back to Russia in 1852, where he worked in his father's company. The company went into bankruptcy in 1859. Alfred and his parents moved back to Sweden, but they left two of his older siblings behind, Robert and Ludvig, to take care of their assets in Russia.

In Sweden, Alfred started experimenting with nitroglycerin in a small laboratory in his father's estate. There was a setback when the factory encountered an explosive accident that killed one of his brothers, Emil. That incident did not deter Alfred; instead, he built and fortified his laboratories against future accidents.

In 1867, Alfred discovered that nitroglycerin could be stabilized and transported when mixed with kieselguhr. Kieselguhr is a light-colored and porous sedimentary rock known as diatomaceous earth. Alfred called the invention dynamite, a name he coined from Greek meaning power. He patented it in Britain in 1867 and the United States in 1868.

Dynamite soon became a product of choice for blasting rocks, tunnels, and canals for road and railway construction. Alfred built factories and incorporated companies all over Europe to manufacture and sell dynamite. In 1875, he developed an improved version of the dynamite: *blasting gelatin.*

Alfred made a fortune from dynamite and ventured into arms manufacturing. He was also prolific in his inventions patenting 355 in his lifetime.

Alfred soon became a man of complex disposition; he created a pacificist reputation but made his fortune from explosives and ammunition manufacture. Unknown to him, the dynamite he invented for industrial use soon developed other uses: military explosives, bombs, and Improvised Electronic Devices (IEDs). These developments led to him being tagged *Agent of Death* in some quarters.

Alfred died of a cerebral hemorrhage in 1896, and he left behind a contentious will that surprised his family. There was a provision that an appointed trust manages the bulk of his estate; the trust should set up a prize and use the proceeds from his estate to fund the different prize categories: Physics, Chemistry, Physiology or Medicine, Literature, and Peace. The first award took place on December 10, 1901—the fifth anniversary of Alfred's death. In 1968, the bank of Sweden instituted another prize in his honor—Economics—bringing the prizes to six.

The Nobel prize is amongst the world's prestigious international awards; the prize money is around SEK 9million ($1.05million) as of 2021 for each category.

When Alfred experimented on nitroglycerin, there was no intention to produce explosives for destructive purposes. The original intent was to invent a better alternative to gunpowder for industrial use. Little did he know that his invention would end up having a sinister use for military bombs and IEDs. Alfred would have been shocked to read his obituary when his older sibling, Ludvig, died in Cannes, France, in

1888. A French tabloid mistook Ludvig for Alfred and published an uncomplimentary remark, *"The merchant of death is dead."* The realization of the negative legacy might have informed his decision to change his will, which has a far-reaching international dimension.

5 HOW TO DEVELOP POSITIVE LEGACY CONSCIOUSNESS

"Through consciousness, our minds have the power to change our planet and ourselves. It is time we heed the wisdom of the ancient indigenous people and channel our consciousness and spirit to tend the garden and not destroy it."

..........*Bruce Lipton*

Everyone needs to develop adequate levels of positive legacy consciousness; it will help to guide one's decision-making and actions. It also aids in forecasting the future impact of one's current actions. After developing positive legacy consciousness, at the point of decision making, you would have been equipped to ask some specific questions: how does my action impact my name, my family name, my immediate environment, my country, my continent, and the world? In addition, it will help stress and bring to the fore your natural selflessness that other competing desires such as immediate enjoyment, ego, shame, and self-centeredness may have overshadowed.

Developing positive legacy consciousness

In decision-making, one should ask some specific questions before making a final decision. I will borrow a leaf from the Rotary club's Four-Way test ethical guide and add a few more tests to it. I am confident that if one applies these rules or principles before making decisions, a positive legacy consciousness will evolve and eventually become one's way of life. I recommend that everyone subjects important decisions to the tests, particularly when the decision affects others. I call it the positive legacy consciousness 7-way test (The 7-way test).

Positive Legacy Consciousness 7-way test (The 7-way test)

When saddled with either individual or collective decision making, one should ask the following questions:

1) Is it the TRUTH?
2) Is it FAIR to all concerned?
3) Will it build GOODWILL and BETTER FRIENDSHIPS?
4) Will it be BENEFICIAL to all concerned?
5) Will HISTORY be kind to me?
6) Are there BETTER ALTERNATIVES?
7) Will my decision make the WORLD a BETTER PLACE?

Exploring the 7-way test criteria

1)   Is it the TRUTH?

TRUTH is one of the critical values for human interaction and co-existence. Sadly, many have abandoned the truth because of the breakdown of societal values or lack of foundational value re-enforcement. The abandonment of the truth has taken different dimensions in individuals and organizations worldwide.

Corporate lies include manufacturing substandard products, changing the expiry dates of products, not packaging the correct quantity, deliberately not delivering on the promised date, creative accounting, and investors' deception.

In government circles, a more powerful government can fund and dispose of a good government in another country to protect the former's interests. For instance, in 1964, during the Vietnam War, it was alleged that the attack on American Warship, MSS Maddox, by North Vietnamese gunboats—the basis for the United States to get involved in the conflict—was a ploy designed to create a moral justification for the United States involvement. If the allegation is true, then the above example is a classic case of the failure of Test 1, the TRUTH test.

It is heartwarming to realize that one can go back to the basic values and re-enforce them in our consciousness and within the people in our circles of influence.

2)   Is it FAIR to all concerned?

In *FAIRness* test, one should look at all the parties directly or indirectly affected by the decision. Are they all treated justly? Is one party favored over the other? A classic instance is a referee in a soccer match. Everyone expects the referee to be an impartial judge who should apply the game's rules to the letter. Imagine how a team and its supporters will feel if they lose a game because of the referee's errors or partial decisions. Suppose a married man has an extramarital affair; three primary parties are directly involved: the man, the wife, and the mistress. While the man and his mistress may be having a good time, the wife is being destroyed emotionally and possibly financially. If the man and his wife have children, chances are that the man will abandon them as well or pay less attention to them because his focus would have shifted to the mistress. The relationship will fail the fairness test; it should be discouraged.

On May 7, 1945, Germany, the primary aggressor in World War II, surrendered, but Japan, a German ally, carried on the fight. In fairness to the United States, the Allied forces gave Japan the opportunity to surrender in the Potsdam declaration of July 26, 1945. However, Japan ignored the ultimatum that led to the atomic bombing of Hiroshima and Nagasaki in August 1945—the bombs decimated both cities. If I subject the action to a fairness test, where I bring in all the parties involved, including the bombed towns' civilian population, can this action pass the fairness test? I doubt it.

3) Will it build *GOODWILL* and *BETTER FRIENDSHIPS?*

In this test, I suggest one takes a more holistic view, as the explanation below proves. The bombing of Hiroshima and Nagasaki was supposed to be a war strategy master class that ended World War II and endorsed the United States as a world superpower, but it created other problems:

i) It brought distrust between the United States and the Soviet Union, another world superpower
ii) It birthed the new arms race for nuclear power

iii)   It birthed the Cold War that lasted for another 45 years; it is still not completely over.

Based on GOODWILL, it is contestable as there are different schools of thought. One school perceives the United States as a world stabilizer and other nations' defender; however, others view the United States as having used innocent Japanese citizens as sacrificial lambs to end the war. It cannot be said to have brought goodwill to other world superpowers; they began to see the United States as a global threat.

On a better friendship test, the Cold War between the United States and the Soviet Union was one of the after-effects of the bombing of Hiroshima and Nagasaki; it stresses the fact that the bombing failed the BETTER FRIENDSHIP test.

4)   *Will it be BENEFICIAL to all concerned?*

I will further subject the atomic bombing of Hiroshima and Nagasaki to the BENEFICIAL to all test. Below are the parties directly affected:

i)   The United States
ii)   The Allied forces
iii) Japanese Emperor and army
iv)   Hiroshima and Nagasaki civilians.

At this point, Germany is no longer in the equation as it had surrendered. I separated the Japanese Emperor and his army from Hiroshima and Nagasaki civilians; the latter bore the brunt of the bombing.

The United States, at this point, can be viewed as the principal actor; it was the planner and the executor of the bombing campaign. Below are the benefits of the action to the United States:

i)   End of the war
ii)   Stoppage of further loss of military personnel and assets
iii) Increase in global stature as the power behind the end of World War II hostilities.

Like the United States, the Allied Forces also enjoyed the same benefits except for the last point.

Regarding the Japanese Emperor and the army, perhaps the bombing made them surrender earlier than planned. Nevertheless, I believe that the defeat of the Japanese military was imminent; the allied forces would have deployed all their military assets to break Japan's resistance since Germany had surrendered. Hiroshima and Nagasaki may have saved Japan from further carnage, suffering, loss of personnel and military assets.

Hiroshima and Nagasaki civilians were the victims of the war, and the sacrificial lambs used to stop World War II. The bombing offered them little or no benefits aside from becoming the cannon fodder to end the war; the residents of both cities faced unimaginable setbacks.

From the above analysis, the BENEFICIAL to all concerned test appears to hang in the balance. Superficially, one could have concluded that the impact of the war on Hiroshima and Nagasaki utterly failed the beneficial to all tests. But wait a minute, what would have happened to both the Allied Forces and Japan if the nuclear bomb did not force Japan to surrender on August 15, 1945? The Japanese military trained a special unit known as the *Kamikaze* to inflict maximum casualty on their enemies even at the expense of their lives. Suppose the war dragged on beyond 6 months; what could have been the attendant cost to the warring parties in terms of personnel and military assets? Visualize the cost and compare it to Hiroshima and Nagasaki.

5)   *Will HISTORY be kind?*

The actors could pass on, but history will continue to judge their actions. HISTORY will not forget the legacy left behind by their actions. Commentaries will continue to be made, especially when such actions affect society; just as I used the Hiroshima and Nagasaki case study over 75 years later. Before making any decision, pause and ask yourself the following question, *how will history judge me?* Still on the case study of the Hiroshima and Nagasaki atomic bombings, how does History judge it? History has not been very kind to the actors involved in several quarters. While some schools of thought view it as the shortest course to ending World War II, others view it as essentially immoral, brutal, inhumane, a crime against humanity, and state terrorism by the United States.

I am from Nigeria, where corruption and looting of state assets are prevalent in people saddled with managing the nation's commonwealth. Also, a sizeable number of citizens get involved in one sharp practice or the other; the most popular ones are *Advance Fee Fraud* and *Internet Fraud*. If the perpetrators of the heinous crimes can ask themselves this simple question, *will history be kind to me for my actions?* And weigh the longer-term implications of their actions against the immediate enjoyment of the proceeds of their illicit activities; I believe that a good number of them will have a rethink.

6)   *Are there BETTER ALTERNATIVES?*

BETTER ALTERNATIVES seek to explore other viable options that will give the same result and leave the action in a positive light. Still on the Hiroshima and Nagasaki example, some schools of thought think that the United States had other options:

i)   Continual aerial bombardment till the Japanese surrender

ii)   Land invasion

iii) Sea blockade

Continual aerial bombardment of Japan was an option the Allied Forces deployed. However, the Japanese had formidable airpower and the added difficulty of the long-range required for the Allied

Forces to hit desired targets in Japan. The Allied Forces attacked Japan on two major fronts, air and through the navy, but the resilience and the indoctrination to die for the Japanese nation kept up the resistance. Furthermore, the Japanese air force had a unit, *Kamikaze*, they trained them to be daring.

The aerial bombardment option would have elongated the war and caused more casualties to the Allied Forces, the Japanese army, and Japanese civilians. I doubt if this would have been a better alternative.

The land invasion was another option available to the Allied Forces. It was an option that the Allied Forces military strategist considered; they dropped it because the estimated casualty on both the Japanese and the Allied forces was unacceptable.

Sea blockade was the third option. Japan is an island country and depends largely on imports for its sustenance. Sea blockade would have meant more deaths and suffering of the Japanese population because of starvation. Moreso, sea blockade could have elongated the war; Japan's resistance may have possibly become fiercer, which could have caused more casualties on both sides.

While there may be arguments in several quarters that the choice of bombing Hiroshima and Nagasaki in Japan was inhumane, the above analysis did not offer us better alternatives.

7)   *Will my decision make the WORLD a BETTER PLACE?*
I will deviate from the Hiroshima and Nagasaki case and use an example that involves virtually everyone: the plastic bottle. In 1973, Nathaniel Wyeth, a Dupont scientist, discovered and patented PET (polyethylene terephthalate) bottles. It was a significant breakthrough

in liquid packaging because it was cheaper, lighter to carry, not easily destroyed, supposed to be recyclable, available, and safe. Companies currently pack bottled water and drinks in PET bottles; however, the breakthrough has soon become a disposal nightmare. Streets in several world cities are now littered, drainage channels blocked, leading to flooding; rivers and seas have become covered with these bottles, threatening the ecosystem.

Has the discovery of PET bottles made the world a better place? Is it not doing more harm than good? For the consumers of products packaged in PET bottles, have you considered where the bottles will end up before you discard the empty container? Is it to block drainage, litter an environment, cover the face of a nearby river, or end up in a recycling plant?

How to implement the 7-way test

Knowing the 7-way test is good, but it will not have the desired effect if not implemented effectively. Below are suggested ways to implement the 7-way test:

a)   *Make it handy*

People make decisions on the spur of the moment. If the 7-way test is not handy, decisions might be concluded without deferring to it. You can make it readily available on the note on your phone and tablet or print a hard copy and place it on your desk. In meetings where you make collective decisions, especially political decisions, the group should collectively subject the favorite decision to the 7-way test.

b)   *Memorize*

Making the 7-way test handy is the first step to memorizing the content. The second step is to get familiar with the keywords: TRUTH, FAIR, GOODWILL and BETTER FRIENDSHIP, BENEFICIAL, HISTORY, BETTER ALTERNATIVES, and WORLD a BETTER PLACE.

The third step is to remember how to use the keywords in each sentence. Since the 7-way test is supposed to be an everyday use material, it should be handy for reference to aid your memorization stage. When transiting or waiting for something, always try to recall them. Again, remembering the keywords is vital to memorizing the content.

c)   *Become a positive legacy ambassador*

The positive legacy ambassador is the person in any group that ensures they do not relegate positive legacy consciousness. My long-term dream is that everyone should be a positive legacy ambassador; that way, positive legacy consciousness becomes inherent in society. There are four suggested qualifications of the legacy ambassador:

i)   Knowing it

ii)   Believing it

iii)   Living it

iv)   Authority.

The positive legacy ambassador(s) in any people group is supposed to familiarize themself with the 7-way test. Everyone, especially the ambassador, should be able to apply the tests without recourse to documented materials in the long run.

Believing the 7-way test is essential to being a positive legacy ambassador. It is simple logic; you cannot sell or drive what you do not support.

Living it is by showing example through your lifestyle; it implies that you are a teacher and a leader in this direction.

The authority could be inherent or delegated. By inherent, I mean your position bestows on you the power to ensure compliance. For instance, the head of a department in an organization can enforce compliance in that department. In a family structure, the father or the mother innately has that level of authority. However, one could delegate the authority to a junior colleague (office) or a child (home) but with adequate power to operate.

6 AREAS TO LEAVE A LEGACY

"The greatest legacy one can pass on to one's children and grandchildren is not money or other material things accumulated in one's life, but rather a legacy of character and faith"

.........Billy Graham

There are several areas to leave a legacy; I will break them into two parts: Foundational and Non-foundational legacies.

The foundational legacies are fundamental; everyone can develop them irrespective of resource, position, or career path. You can build foundational legacies as soon as you have developed positive legacy consciousness. Foundational legacy areas are character, integrity, network/relationships, health, and spirituality.

The non-foundational legacies are a function of one's opportunities and circumstances. We are all unique in our ways and positioned differently to leave legacies in these areas. The non-foundational legacies areas are knowledge, wealth, sports, music/writing/arts, power/politics, and humanity/philanthropy.

Foundational Legacies

These are the basic legacies; one can develop them irrespective of circumstances and opportunities. Foundational legacy development should begin as soon as you can appreciate positive legacy consciousness. The great news is that you do not need special resources to cultivate them. As earlier listed, the foundational legacies areas are character, integrity, network/relationships, health, and spirituality.

Character

Aside from one's physical look, character is another attribute that individualizes a person. Every individual is unique in their ways; while there may be similarities, no two people will exhibit precisely the same character. We all have positive and negative character traits; the responsibility of everyone, especially influencers, is to identify, nurture, accentuate, and continually reinforce positive character traits. At the same time, one should identify and diminish negative character traits. When a person of influence leaves behind positive character in an environment, it becomes an operational culture that permeates that environment. The same goes for negative character traits. Examples of positive character traits are adventure, cooperation, devotion, discipline, determination, fairness, faithfulness, generosity, hard work, integrity, kindness, loving, loyalty, sincerity, optimism, patience, peacefulness, persistence, personability, and tolerance. Some of the listed character traits are important in shaping organizations. When an organization identifies what makes them unique, it is documented as its values that every employee imbibes. Examples of the attributes that feed into an organization's culture are cooperation, fairness, hard work, integrity, openness, and optimism. Some positive character attributes could be more suited to personal interactions with others, such as adventurousness, generosity, loving, tolerance, and being personable. Others may be more suited to a person's wellbeing and personal development, such as discipline, hard work, determination, persistence, and focus.

Positive character identification, development, and reinforcement

One should identify, cultivate, maintain, and accentuate positive character in what I term continuous positive character reinforcement. If not done, the positive character could diminish over time, and your negative character may overshadow the positive character. The devolution into negative character may not be intentional; it could sometimes be circumstantial. Age, loss of loved ones, job loss, environmental influences, enervating circumstances, and rejection could be the root causes of one's negative character development. Nevertheless, I am confident that continuous positive character reinforcement will turn the tide and bring one back to a positive character default setting.

At the early stage of my marriage, a little less than two decades ago, if my wife complains about any person, I inadvertently find a way to explain the person's actions in a positive light. I give excuses without hearing the inciter's side of the story, such as maybe the provoker probably woke up on the wrong side, likely acted based on incomplete information, or may need to be supported. Somehow, I find an excuse that makes the complainant feel better about the other person's actions. Often, my response changes the complainant's mood from pain and revenge to understanding and support. Fast forward to fifteen years later, my wife called my attention to the fact that I no longer defend people; instead, I join in complaining about them. My earlier disposition in that aspect was subconscious; nonetheless, I lost it. Luckily, my wife noted the change and discussed it with me. Unknown to me, that character attribute positively affected her. I would have devolved from a peacemaker to a nagger if she did not remind me that I had lost such an emulable attribute. While thinking of it, I realized that people's positive character traits might be lost because they did not recognize, nurture, maintain, accentuate, and reinforce them. There must be ways of handling these attributes to avoid losing them unintentionally because they will define your personality and legacy.

I suggest below steps to identifying, nurturing, accentuating, and reinforcing positive character traits:

- Two-level open-ended positive character list
- Two-level structured positive character list
- Comprehensive list of positive character
- Action plan for positive character development and nurturing
- Accentuating and reinforcing positive characters
- Scheduled review

Two-level open-ended positive character list

S/ No	Criteria *(List positive character and tick level beside as appropriate)*	Scores 0-5, (0=Low, 5=High level)					
		0	1	2	3	4	5
1							
2							
3							
4							
5 ...							
10							

One should develop this list at two levels; the first should be a self-appraisal, while another person should do the second. The person to do it should have an appreciable knowledge of your character.

Two-level structured positive character list

S/No	Criteria	Scores 0-5, (0=Low, 5=High level)					
		0	1	2	3	4	5
	(A) Personal development attributes						
1	Discipline,						
2	Determination,						
3	Devotion						
4	Hard work						
	(B) Association attributes						
5	Fairness						
6	Faithfulness						
7	Generosity						
8	Loyalty						

The two-level structured positive character list is like the two-level open-ended positive character list. The difference is that the two-level structured list provides a comprehensive list from where one could choose. The structured list's advantage over the open-ended list is that it is easier to identify specific positive character traits that one may likely omit in the open-ended character list, especially the ones you could not describe correctly in the earlier list.

Comprehensive list of positive character

The comprehensive list of positive personal character is a product of the first two exercises (the two-level open-ended positive character list and the two-level guided positive character list). It is a summarized report sheet that gives you a picture of your positive character. It shows two sets of positive character traits, first, the ones that need to be accentuated and continually re-enforced, and second, the desirable ones that need to be nurtured, accentuated, and continuously reinforced. Since the list is comprehensive, I advise that you arrange the attributes in diminishing order of importance. That way, the ones you believe that you need most will not get lost in the crowd. I arranged the guided schedule alphabetically; I did not attach any importance to it. Every individual is unique in their ways and views each attribute's essence differently. For clarity, I advise you to develop two comprehensive lists; the first is the list of identified positive attributes you have developed. You need to nurture, accentuate and reinforce them continuously, and the second is a comprehensive list of positive attributes you desire to develop, nurture, accentuate, and reinforce.

Developed positive character list

S/ No	Criteria	Scores 0-5, (0=Low, 5=High level)						
		0	1	2	3	4	5	Remarks
	(A) Personal development attributes							
1	Discipline,							
2	Determination,							
3	Devotion							
4	Hard work							
	(B) Association attributes							
5	Fairness							
6	Faithfulness							
7	Generosity							
8	Loyalty							

Desirable positive character lists

S/No	Criteria	Scores 0-5, (0=Low, 5=High level)						
		0	1	2	3	4	5	Remarks
	(A) Personal development attributes							
1	Discipline							
2	Determination							
3	Devotion							
4	Hard work							
	(B) Association attributes							
5	Fairness							
6	Faithfulness							
7	Generosity							
8	Loyalty							

Resolving conflicts in the grading of the positive character list

There will likely be a conflict between your grading and your assessor's grading while developing the positive character list. There are three possible grading outcomes:

- The same grading
- A slim gap in grading
- A wide gap in grading.

The same grading means that you and your assessor agree on the attribute, implying no conflict in opinion.

If there is a narrow grading gap, it means that you and your assessor feel almost the same way, but the grading will be different because of the inherently subjective nature of gradings. To align the two gradings, you should take the average of the two and round them down. Rounding down will be more realistic; rounding up is somewhat optimistic.

Where there is a wide gap in grading, I suggest that you seek a second opinion, take the average of the two closest views, and round down.

Action plan for positive character development and nurturing
After completing the comprehensive list, the most pressing attributes that need development and nurturing should have become clear. I advise that you do not pick too many attributes simultaneously for nurturing. However, you can merge related attributes that require the same set of actions to develop. Below are suggested ways to develop and nurture the desirable attributes:

- Association strategy
- Mentoring
- Training
- Books

In *association strategy*, identify a person or persons with the attribute you desire to develop and befriend them. For instance, my wife's friend—Dotun—they attended the same college. My first conversation with her made me realize my negative disposition. She is courteous, humble, and positive in her conversations; she always says the right words in seemingly desperate situations. I advised my wife to be close to her. Surrounding yourself with people with the attributes you desire can help you assimilate and imbibe those attributes consciously and subconsciously. The same also applies to undesirable traits—stay away from negative influences.

Mentoring is close to association strategy. In mentoring, you learn from somebody ahead of you in your career or age. In association strategy, the person you are to imbibe the attribute from might be your junior, at the same level, or ahead of you in career/age. Essentially, the association is informal, and the associate may be unaware of your motive for maintaining constant contact. Mentoring is more formal than association strategy, and the mentor should know your motive. The mentor should work with you to achieve the set goal.

Training is another great avenue to learn and develop the required attributes in an area of interest. It can directly address the area in question within a short period. You should invest time and resources to enable you to achieve your aim. Look out for training in these areas, ensure you attend, participate in the class activities, and form a network of people seeking the same attribute.

Reading books that address the attribute in question is equally effective. The more you read about the attribute, the more knowledgeable you will become, and in no time, you can train and mentor others in that area.

Accentuating and reinforcing positive character

Accentuation is to make an attribute more noticeable. An unaccentuated positive character will eventually diminish. I liken it to a skill set that was acquired but not put to practice; over time, the acquirer will lose grip of the skill set. Let us take showing love as an example; there are several opportunities: family, neighborhood, office, and the less privileged. Be intentional about reflecting your positive character.

Scheduled review

After developing a comprehensive list of positive personal character and designing action plans (association, mentoring, training, and books), you should create a scheduled review of the progress made. It is not enough to plan; you need to execute and measure your progress. Depending on the time available and the urgency of the attributes, you can choose between one year and five years to schedule a review. Below are suggested review processes:

- Keep a copy of the comprehensive positive character list in a retrievable form. It can be a hard or soft copy
- Choose a review period between one year and five years. I recommend two years, preferably at the end of the second year
- Repeat a fresh process of developing a comprehensive character list
- Compare both lists and measure progress
- Identify the most effective action plans and design future action plans
- Repeat the process in the future as appropriate.

Steps to identifying and correcting negative character

One can also exhibit negative character traits. It is essential to identify personal negative character traits and consciously diminish them. The reason is that one's negative attributes are more likely to be accentuated than positive attributes. Bad news, they say, travels fast. It is sad to note that most people live in self-denial and find it difficult to own up to their negative character traits. Negative character traits include abrasiveness, anger, caustic, cruelty, dishonesty, disloyalty, disrespectfulness, greed, tardiness, laziness, maliciousness, meanness, mercilessness, narcissism, rudeness, impatience, indulgence, obnoxious, pessimism, pettiness, procrastination, quarrelsome, selfishness, vengefulness, and unkindness.

Below are two recommended steps to identifying one's negative attributes:

I)   Self-review
II) External review

Self-review

In self-review, take some time and review the attributes you have acknowledged that are not good enough in your personal life: laziness, procrastination, pessimism, and indulgence, as well as your association with others: quarrelsomeness, impatience, and rudeness.

A guide to self-review

I recommend a detailed self-review guide to avoid missing out on some essential negative character traits.

S/No	Criteria	Scores 0-5, (0=Low, 5=High level)					
		0	1	2	3	4	5
	(A) Personal development attributes						
1	Indecisiveness						
2	Lack of focus						
3	Laziness						
4	Indulgence						
	(B) Association attributes						
5	Maliciousness						
6	Abrasiveness						
7	Cruelty						
8	Dishonesty						

Using a grading of 0-5, zero means that you have no noticeable trace of such a negative attribute, while five implies that the negative character attribute is high. I regard any score of three or above to be high; one should give the attribute attention. Note that the list in the schedule above is not exhaustive.

External review

After an objective personal review, I will still recommend an external review because one's opinion may be myopic and self-deluding. Some people could know you better than you think you know yourself, and your opinion may differ from what people think of you. The external review should be the balancing factor to correct undesirable attributes.

Criteria for choosing a review partner

Consider the following criteria when choosing an external review partner:

i)   Good knowledge

ii) Objectivity

iii) Reasonable independence

The review partner should know you enough to identify hidden attributes that need attention. The reviewer's objectivity is necessary; reasonable independence will affect objectivity. Four groups of people readily come to my mind that could meet good knowledge and reasonable independence criteria: one's spouse, a colleague at the same level in the office, your parents, and your siblings—especially your older siblings. Anyone that depends on you for sustenance is not qualified to play the role.

During the review, I suggest that you listen attentively, jot down as many comments as possible, and not argue with the reviewer. Remember that the aim is to identify your character flaws in order to take corrective action(s). If you want to explain some of your actions, ensure the reviewer finishes because the essence is to understand how people view you. If you disagree with the reviewer's opinion, seek a second opinion. Richard Branson once said, *"The least you can get out of a second opinion is that it will confirm the first opinion."*

Methods of external review

i) Open-ended questions
ii) Structured questions
iii) Hybrid

In an open-ended question, you can ask questions like, *What attributes in me would you have wished I changed?* Or *What attributes in me do you find obnoxious?* The advantage of this method is that it gives the respondent the freedom to express himself as he wishes; however, where the respondent lacks the right words to express himself succinctly, the objective may be defeated.

In the structured type, list possible character flaws based on personal perception. You may also include those flaws you are not falling short of in order to assess the respondent's objectivity and determine how much the person knows you.

The hybrid style is a combination of both structured lists and open-ended questions. The first part should be the structured list, and the second part, open-ended. I suggest that you do not perform the review immediately after administering the questionnaire; this will give the respondent enough time to respond thoroughly.

Correcting negative character traits

Below are possible steps to take towards correcting a negative character:

- Root cause identification

- Design corrective strategy

After identifying the negative character, the next step is to identify the root cause. You need to know whether the trait is hereditary (traceable to your family) or environmentally induced? The next stage is to design a corrective strategy. For example, if the undesirable character is hereditary, it may just require the development of the consciousness to depart from that default character setting. You may need to seek a specialist (psychologist) or a counselor if you cannot manage it.

For environmentally induced character traits, including association, you may need to change your environment or your association and locate environments/associations that will help you to overcome the undesirable character.

Character is one area available to all to leave a legacy. The impact will vary depending on a person's circle of influence. One cannot equate the impact of the Prime Minister or the President on a country to that of a civil servant, but they all have the opportunity to leave a legacy. Irrespective of the circle of influence, one should leave a positive legacy because the positively influenced person might later end up in a bigger stage where he can have a larger circle of influence. For instance, John D. Rockefeller, the biggest American oil magnate in the twentieth century, was influenced positively by his devout and strict mother and negatively by his cunning father. These two influences later played significant roles in his business dealings and personal life. His monopolistic tendencies and the killing of competition is traceable to his father's cunning behavior, while his generosity and dedication to spirituality are linked to his mother.

One may think that his current actions may be influencing only a child, but that child could become the country's future President. Thus, your legacy at the lowest level of the family now may play out in the entire nation or globally in the next generation.

Integrity

Integrity should typically be part of character, but because of its unassailable importance in legacy, I thought it should stand on its own in this chapter to give it the attention it deserves. However, that does not change it as a character attribute. Integrity is the quality of being honest and having moral principles; it connotes that your word is your bond. In business, integrity demands that you deliver whatever you promised (time, quality, and quantity). A few countries and companies are known globally to provide high-quality products, and the reverse is the case in a host of others. Aliko Dangote, the richest man in Africa as of 2021, once said that he could joke with anything but not his name (he meant integrity).

In politics, officeholders with integrity play by the rules and do not act in manners that could soil their names. Corruption and perpetuation in the office are the opposite behaviors of politicians with integrity. If we have people with integrity holding political offices, they will base their decisions on the constitution and fairness instead of nepotism, which is predominant in several countries. The former President of Chad, Late Idriss Deby, who ruled Chad for 30 years, was fatally injured by rebels while commanding troops on the frontline on April 20, 2021. His son, 37year old Mahamat Idriss Deby, immediately assumed office following the suspension of the constitution by the army. The Chadian constitution stipulated that the parliament speaker takes charge of the country for 40 days upon the President's death. A transition government is put in place until they hold elections. The above action undermines the sacrosanctity of the constitution and questions the integrity of the Chadian ruling class.

Lack of integrity breeds unfairness leading to dissent from the populace. The extreme result of dissent is internal strife and civil war. In business, where the products from a particular country or company cannot meet the acceptable standard, it could lead to a bad reputation (legacy) and the loss of market share to countries/companies with better quality. In relationships, loss of integrity comes with the loss of trust, and your audience may resort to cross-checking every statement you make.

Finally, lack of integrity breeds mistrust and strive in families: one of the primary causes of divorce in marriages. In 1997, Austrian-born former California governor, Arnold Schwarzenegger, fathered a son, Joseph, through their housekeeper, Mildred Patricia Baena; he kept it away from his wife, Maria Shriver, for over 14 years. It was alleged that Maria's knowledge of the affair led to the couple's separation in 2011 and eventual divorce in 2017.

Network/Relationships

In chapter one, understanding legacy, one of the dictionary definitions of legacy is *"a candidate for membership in an organization."* I further explained it as *"certain privileges one is entitled through a close relative who has had or still has a relationship with the organization. An example is a parent being an alumnus of an organization (company or school) gives the child a distinct edge in being accepted into that organization, especially if the referenced person has an excellent track record."* In the above definition, I based the legacy the dependent enjoys on a relationship, or an association left behind by the predecessor: the root legacy.

We all interact with different people and organizations as we engage in our various endeavors. We should build lasting relationships along with our growth; these relationships may be invaluable to us and our dependents in the future. One may not be able to bequeath assets of high value, but at least bequeath good networks and relationships. Technology has made it possible to build and maintain networks remotely. Group chats have been created on various social media platforms; it has resurrected several forgotten networks. I attended a high school briefly over thirty years ago, and out of the blue, I received a call from one of the chat group administrators that she wanted to add me to the chat group. I could only recollect a few of the members; however, I got positive feelings from the reunion because it brought back the memory of some events in my adolescence stage.

We should not limit the networks to banters and chats alone but are advised to share valuable information and develop causes of common interest. Networks are forums to support each other, especially as we grow older. The high school I graduated from created a chat group; shortly after, they talked about carrying out developmental projects in our alma mater. In most of the chat groups I belong to, very few people are usually active, and in no time, they take over the leadership roles in the chat groups. If we have relevant skills that the group needs, let us not hesitate to offer them. Networks are promising avenues to showcase our talents and get referrals; members know you and can vouch for you. They also belong to other groups that you cannot access directly; the reach of these networks could be exponential if properly harnessed. We should not underestimate their potential. Nonetheless, social media networks have their challenges; the distraction and time to maintain them could be daunting.

One could belong to several networks: high school, college, professional, past and present office(s), spiritual, neighborhood, and clubs. The contacts in our phones are another excellent source of networks. To keep the contacts active, we can use the calendar on our phones to set reminders about events concerning our contacts such as birthdays, anniversaries, and engagements.

Building relationships

Technology has helped us to develop and maintain networks, but it does not entirely build our relationships. We may belong to a host of networks yet remain inconspicuous. One needs to understand how to cultivate and maintain relationships to take full advantage of the networks that are made possible by technology. Below is a list of steps that will help us develop lasting relationships:

- Be intentional about building relationships
- Love people
- Be approachable
- Be approaching
- Overcome fear of rejection
- Be persistent
- Be willing to help
- Be a go-to person
- Do not be a parasite

I will liken being intentional about building a relationship to a salesperson on a sales call. If the salesperson spends the entire day with the client or prospective client without asking for the deal, he has just wasted his time. When interacting with others, note that the long-term goal is to build a lasting relationship. Be intentional about the actions that would enable a long-lasting relationship.

Love people irrespective of how they are: short, tall, educated, uneducated, obese, or colored. Aside from the atheists that think otherwise, the same God created us differently. Christians believe that God is omniscient; He does not make mistakes, so who are we to question His creations?

Being approachable is a quality everyone that intends to build relationships should have. Approachability requires a neat and friendly disposition for physical contact, and in remote meetings, tone and choice of words play essential roles.

A relationship builder approaches people; he does not wait for others to come to him. The relationship builder is the one that usually drops the ice breaker in meetings.

Most people who intend to create relationships face the fear of rejection. A relationship builder should overcome the fear; the reality is that human beings don't bite.

Some people are naturally reluctant to meet new people and are also resistant initially; however, a relationship builder that persists will eventually break that barrier.

A relationship builder should always be willing to help others; he should strive to become a go-to person.

Being a go-to person requires that he should be knowledgeable in several areas and be available for others.

A relationship builder does not use his relationships for personal gain without giving out something in return. Do not be a parasite that always receives without giving.

Building relationships with people of different cultures

The above generic steps should work in several instances in building relationships; nevertheless, they may not work if the person you are attempting to develop the relationship with is of a different culture. Below are suggested steps that should help in breaking possible barriers occasioned by cultural differences:

- Seek to understand the person's culture
- Identify and appreciate the cultural nuances
- Understand the person's attachment to culture
- Strike a balance.

In understanding a person's culture, you need to know about their belief systems; they may differ from yours.

Each culture has its nuances; some are subtle, while others are obvious. Understanding these differences will help you accept and relate to the uniqueness of the person's culture.

While people's cultures may vary, their attachment differs from person to person; thus, somebody born and groomed in a village may not have the same attachment to culture as somebody born in the city or a foreign land.

In relating with people of different cultures, especially in a group, it is necessary to balance it. One should aim at a middle ground where you do not ignore or offend the minority cultures while relating with the dominant cultures in the group.

Health

One legacy that we often ignore but is of great significance is good health practices. Many people have died untimely because they lacked the knowledge to treat their bodies correctly. As one gets older, the body begins to show the impact of our lifestyles.

Several systems and organs make up the human body. We should know how the body systems work and pass down the knowledge to enable us and people within our circle of influence to live a longer and healthier life. There are seventy-eight primary organs in the human body; each performs different functions, and most depend on each other. When one organ is not performing its function(s) properly, it usually affects the entire body. I will not be listing all the organs here but will explain the role of some of them below:

- The skin is the largest organ in the body; its primary function is to maintain body temperature

- The brain stores information that enables thinking, decisions, and response to stimuli

- The heart is the body's engine room; it pumps oxygenated blood to the body and receives deoxygenated blood

- The kidney is the filtration machine of the body; it removes salt and water from the body, produces urine, and an enzyme called rennin that helps to regulate blood pressure

- The liver produces the bile that is sent to the stomach for digestion; it is also in charge of converting and storing sugar

- The primary function of the pancreas is to produce insulin that regulates blood sugar; it also helps in digestion by producing enzymes.

The organs are formed from birth; they are expected to continue to perform their functions until death. It appears that God did not design the organs to be replaced; nonetheless, medicine has advanced to a stage where some of them have been successfully transplanted: the heart, kidney, liver, lungs, pancreas, intestine, thymus, and uterus. Before advising on transplanting procedures, several factors should be considered: the extent of damage, cost, availability of organ and surgical expertise, and other risks assessment.

We need to understand how these organs and systems in our bodies work and consciously act to protect them. One can take several steps to ensure we live our lives healthily and educate others as well. I am particularly interested in the younger ones; early consciousness of healthy living will go a long way to avoid debilitating sicknesses. Below are recommended actions that will help in living a healthy life:

- Access to safe water
- Drink enough water daily
- Avoid living in a polluted environment, especially exposure to carbon monoxide
- Avoid alcohol or heavy drinking
- Avoid smoking
- Exercise often
- Avoid oily and fried food
- Reduce red meat intake
- Eat more fish
- Reduce salt to the barest minimum
- Avoid excess sugar
- Avoid excess carbohydrates
- Avoid late-night food
- Eat the fruit of the season and vegetables
- Avoid exposure to different sexual partners
- Involve in activities to balance sedentary lifestyle
- Do medical check-ups as often as practicable.

Safe drinking water is essential for our healthy living; unsafe water could expose one to cholera, gastrointestinal illness, river blindness, reproductive defects, and cancer. For the organs in our bodies to function properly, health officials recommend that we drink an adequate quantity of clean and safe water every day. The amount of water one needs depends on body size, health condition, activity, and climate. For instance, the quantity of water one requires in summer should be more than in winter; however, the American National Academy of Medicine (NAM) recommends three liters per day for men and two liters for women. Water intake has several health benefits: it helps to regulate the body temperature, lubricates the joints, delivers oxygen through the blood, helps to regulate blood pressure, helps in weight loss, and prevents kidney damage.

Exposure to carbon monoxide reduces the blood's ability to carry oxygen that the body needs. A high concentration of carbon monoxide could kill in a few minutes.

Excess intake of alcohol causes Alcohol Use Disorder (AUD). AUD has a long-term adverse effect on vital organs: the brain, the heart, liver, pancreas, and immune system.

Cigarette smoking has several adverse effects. Cigarettes negatively impact the skin, eyes, circulatory system, respiratory system, reproductive system, and exposure to cancer risk. Most countries' health authorities insist on putting a warning on every packet sold that those who smoke cigarettes are likely to die young.

Exercising has several health benefits: it helps in muscle tone, controls body sugar and weight, reduces the risk of heart disease, and helps in mental health and mood.

Most oily and fried food contains an excess amount of bad cholesterol, LDL, that clogs the wall of blood vessels and increases the risk of high blood pressure.

Although debatable, the consensus is that a high intake of red meat exposes one to a higher risk of cancer, diabetes, heart disease, and premature death. It is traceable to the high content of saturated fat found in most red meat. Saturated fat is high in cholesterol; a moderate intake is advisable.

Fish is rich in protein and omega-3 fatty acids; they are good for the heart and brain. The body does not produce omega-3 fatty acids.

According to the World Health Organization (WHO), an average person consumes more salt (sodium) than the body needs. An average person consumes 9-12 grams per day instead of the recommended less than 5 grams per day. WHO asserts that if we reduce salt intake to the recommended amount, yearly world death could reduce by 2.5 million. High sodium consumption increases the risk of high blood pressure, cardiovascular disease, coronary heart disease, and stroke.

Sugar is tasty to the tongue, but that is where the fun ends. Excess sugar in the body has several side effects: tooth decay, increased body weight, kidney damage, heart disease, skin aging, and arthritis. The most common effect is the impact on the pancreas; it forces it to keep producing insulin to stabilize the excess sugar in the body until the pancreas cannot cope anymore. The continued pressure on the pancreas could lead to type 2 diabetes.

Carbohydrate is the primary energy source in the body; however, the excess may cause problems for the human body. The digestive system breaks down carbohydrates into glucose, the primary energy source in the body. The liver stores excess glucose, and too much of it causes several problems: low energy, craving for food, weakened immune system, obesity, and insomnia.

Late-night food is a habit many have developed over time because of either indiscipline or lifestyle. Giving the digestive system work to do while preparing to rest is unsuitable for the body. Late-night food has several adverse effects: weight gain, increased acidity, increased blood sugar, obesity, and poor memory.

In Nigeria, different fresh fruits and food come out each season; It should be the same for several other countries. Ensure you take advantage of the fruits and food; they have different health benefits. Fresh maize that is rich in fiber and Vitamin B is available from April to December in Nigeria; orange that is rich in Vitamin C is available between September and March every year; apple that Nigerians import from South Africa is rich in Vitamin C, K, and potassium is available all year round; and vegetables, an excellent source of Vitamin B, folate, copper, magnesium, zinc, and phosphorous are available all year round, but they are more in the rainy season.

Exposure to different sexual partners has both psychological and health implications. Psychologically, it could lead to disappointment, distrust from one's partner, and at the extreme, the mental health of the victimized partner. Medically, one could be exposed to sexually transmitted diseases (STDs). While there are several curable STDs, four are still not curable: Hepatitis B, Herpes, Human Immune Virus (HIV), and Human Papilloma Virus (HPV); the only advisable solution is to remain faithful to one sexual partner.

Most jobs are sedentary; computing and digitalization have made it possible to do several remotely. People now work from their homes; commuting to and from work is gradually tapering. Nevertheless, the development poses another challenge: a sedentary lifestyle. A sedentary lifestyle brings several health challenges: obesity, waist pain, neck pain, and mental disorder. One can take advantage of the following lifestyle changes to counter the adverse effects of a sedentary lifestyle: walking to work, taking the stairway instead of the elevator, using health watches to monitor your activities, gardening, and DIY (Do It Yourself); there are a lot of activities you can do yourself that will help you exercise: cooking, washing, cleaning surroundings and ironing.

Carrying out the above-recommended activities will not replace the need to have regular comprehensive medical check-ups at least yearly; it will help identify hidden ailment(s) that can be nipped in the bud.

I lost both of my parents at the good age of seventy; the last ten years of their lives were challenging health-wise. My father suffered Type2 diabetes, and my mother had high blood pressure that led to a partial stroke. My parents never practiced healthy living. Although my father had a college degree, he did not develop healthy living consciousness. They never had a blood pressure monitor or a glucometer to monitor their blood sugar levels. They ate late at night and often more than the quantity of carbohydrates their bodies needed.

My wife and I have started practicing healthy living, but I think we are a bit late; we are over our middle 40s. The great news is that our children who are in their teens have started imbibing healthy living culture. The sugar jar is no longer getting used up as it used to; butter and bread consumption has reduced considerably. We now cook yam and plantains without salt, and our children can eat them; we cook our rice and beans with minimal salt. We no longer refrigerate our drinking water and have eliminated red meat from our menu. Our source of protein now is mainly eggs, chicken, and fish.

Another benefit of healthy living is that it reduces your spending; it almost eliminates impulsive buying and improves your health. If my parents had developed healthy lifestyles, I would have imbibed it earlier, and I could have avoided my youthful wastefulness. I believe that I would have had better health. Barely two years ago, during the COVID-19 lockdown, my house was filled with sugar, salt, butter, bread, and carbs.

Spirituality

Spirituality is the recognition of a divine being that one is devoted. The divine being is usually unseen, but the devotee has a palpable connection. Spirituality demands discipline, dedication, trust, and total obedience to the divine being's dictates and directives. Often, these directives and rules of the divine being are at variance with the human desires that are essentially hedonistic.

In *Christianity*, we view God as a supreme being and the creator of the earth and the universe. Adherents see the Bible as the spoken word of God and the rule book handed to us through inspired men of God. The Bible explains how the earth came to be and the relationship between God and man. There are several directives embedded in the Bible that adherents should observe. Examples are fellowship with others known as brethren in Christianity parlance, abstinence from sex before marriage, and non-committing of sins: lies, not getting drunk, and no backbiting. Other principles such as faith gives you confidence that a divine being will intervene, even when it does not appear to be logically or scientifically possible in what is known as a miracle. Also, fallen angels headed by the devil, Heaven, and hell are topics of interest in the Bible. There are several sects within Christianity, each with its beliefs and practices—doctrines. For instance, the Catholic church demands a total dedication of a select few to the service of God, and they are to remain single throughout their lifetime. They are called priests or Reverends and are expected to live above board; other sects do not require this level of dedication to become a priest or pastor.

In *Islam,* adherents believe in one supreme God: Allah (SWT), and his messenger: prophet Muhammad (PBUH), whom angel Gabriel (Jibril) spoke to and handed down the Quran during their meetings in cave Hira. Islam devotees are called Muslims; their holy book is the Quran. The Quran contains 114 chapters called surah and conveys Allah's instruction to Muhammad (PBUH) through angel Gabriel. Islam is based on five primary pillars:

- *Shahada,* a declaration to faith in Allah (SWT) and the belief in prophet Muhammad (PBUH)
- *Salat,* to pray five times daily
- *Zakat,* giving alms to the needy
- *Sawm,* to observe fasting at Ramadhan
- *Hajj,* to make a holy pilgrimage to Mecca at least once in a Muslim's lifetime.

In *traditional worship,* adherents believe in a supreme God who communicates with them through a priest; he offers sacrifices to the divine being on behalf of the people. Each geographical region has its different type of traditional worship and is independent of each other.

To leave a spiritual legacy, you need to take your relationship with the divine being you are devoted to a notch higher than an average adherent: obedience, knowledge, and association. In addition, you need to attain some apparent supernatural abilities that may not be achievable by a regular adherent.

Non-Foundational legacies

As explained earlier at the onset of this chapter, non-foundational legacies are not accessible by everyone. It is usually a product of one's uniqueness, resources, circumstances, and desires. They include knowledge, wealth, sports, music/writing/arts, power/politics, and humanity/philanthropy.

Knowledge

Knowledge could be in the form of unique skills, know-how, specialized information, or a deep understanding of a subject. The Cable News Network (CNN) usually runs a program, *The 100 Club*, where they showcase companies that have operated for one hundred years or over. Often, these companies operate in specialized fields, and the knowledge of the production process is passed down from one generation to another. One of the companies they always showcased, *Tabasco Pepper Sauce*, was founded by Edmund McIlhenny in 1868, over 150 years ago, as of 2021. In the narration, the company executive asserts that Edmund McIlhenny produced 350,000 bottles of the pepper sauce in his lifetime, but as of 2021, they produce 150,000 bottles per day. It means that the company's current output in two days is what the founder could produce in his lifetime. The preceding narrative is a classic example of previous knowledge continually improved for the good of both the knowledge custodians and the world. The Tabasco instance brings to my consciousness the Japanese terminology, *Kaizen*. *Kaizen* means continuous improvement or change for the better. It is a philosophy that is embedded in Japanese business and operational culture. The consciousness of continually improving the company's processes involves all employees; it is the organization's responsibility to create an enabling environment for it to foster. In the Tabasco case, in 1869, Edmund McIlhenny produced only 658 bottles of the sauce; he had only one flavor and was shipping only to New Orleans, Louisiana, United States. As of 2021, they produced 150,000 bottles per day in eight different flavors and exported them to over

195 countries worldwide. The company has the ambition of staying for the next 150 years.

As of 2021, Tabasco Pepper Sauce still practices some of the knowledge developed by Edmund Mcllhenny in the production process; the little red stick used by farm hands to measure the pepper's ripeness is still in use.

I can break knowledge into two categories:

I)   Open Knowledge
II) Closed knowledge

Open knowledge

Open knowledge is available to the public. Knowledge and information shared in books and academic journals come under this category. In 1887, Heinrich Rudolf Hertz discovered the Photoelectric effect that Philipp Lenard further explained in 1902. They found a relationship between light and electricity when the light falls on an object; however, they could not explain the relationship. In 1905, Albert Einstein explained the relationship by deriving a formula that solved the puzzle. The explanation earned Albert Einstein a Nobel Prize for physics in 1921. All these were possible because it was open knowledge; each scientist did their bit and made their findings public until Einstein resolved the puzzle.

Closed Knowledge

I gave the example of Edmund Mcllhenny of the Tabasco Pepper Sauce at the beginning of this subheading. In this case, the inventor keeps the knowledge and usually patents it. The public will enjoy the knowledge output through its products, but the production process remains a trade secret of the founding organization. Improvements in the production process are usually within the confines of the organization. In some instances, the production process and brand name are given out to third parties in a franchise, where the franchisee uses the brand name and production process for an agreed fee.

Knowledge also includes computing. For example, developing programs that solve common problems fall into the closed knowledge category.

Wealth

Bequest of wealth is usually the most common legacy; it could be in cash, estates, luxury goods, and holdings in companies. The typical expectation and practice are that the bequeather passes on the wealth to dependents. While dependents bequest has become a tradition, there are schools of thought that believe that the practice does not do justice to the common good of humankind. Leaving enormous assets to one's dependents could harm the endowment's beneficiaries; it appears to inhibit their creativity and the desire to work hard in a sizeable number of cases. According to a CNN report, 60% of bequeathed wealth disappears during the first generation; 90% are gone by the second generation. Michael Klepper and Robert Gunther gave a classic example in their book, *The Wealthy 100,* where they traced the wealth of Cornelius Vanderbilt. Cornelius made his fortunes from railway and shipping in the nineteenth century; they valued him at about $200billion in current times. By the twentieth century, there was no millionaire left in his family.

The bequeathers mean well for the family by leaving their assets, but they fail to pass on an essential primary skill: wealth management. Usually, the bequeather's case is a rag to riches story, and he would have developed the requisite wealth management skills along with the wealth acquisition. However, they are not often able to pass on the skill. The bequeathers do not realize that they do not share common experiences with their dependents, so they frequently have different motivations from their heirs.

Based on the above example, one would question how best to bequeath wealth: what, how much, and under what condition? One of the suggested ways to deal with this challenge is for the bequeather to pass on the assets and leave explicit instructions and guidelines on managing these assets. The snag in this suggestion is that what may seem right in the twentieth century may not be right in the twenty-first century. For instance, one of the significant philanthropist gestures of Andrew Carnegie was to build libraries all over the United States and around the world. In the nineteenth century, that was a great idea. I doubt if that idea is still that great now; with the advent of information technology, libraries are increasingly moving to laptops, tablets, and phones. The attraction to public libraries was primarily to access books and a serene environment for reading, but currently, several books have become virtual. Covid-19 protocols have also limited the desire to convene in public, thereby reducing the attractiveness of public libraries. The exchange of hard copies of books and use of the library facilities could go against Covid-19 protocols. A possible solution to the situation is to make the directive open-ended. Instead of instructing the building of libraries, I believe that access to information and learning resources would be a better directive. The implementers will then design an appropriate infrastructure to suit specific environments and situations. Libraries may still be relevant in certain parts of the world, but I believe that access to power, gadgets, and Wi-Fi will be more appropriate in most parts of the world right now.

Sports

Sports combine innate abilities, constant training and development, a disciplined lifestyle, and providence to create a legacy status. It entails setting an almost unassailable standard that everyone in that sport aspires to beat. To create a legacy status, one must separate self from the pack. Several individuals in different sports globally have been able to leave legacies or are in the process.

In basketball, Michael Jordan stood out from the pack; in soccer, Pele, Ronaldo, and Lionel Messi are head above shoulders from the rest, and they have scored unimaginable goals; Pele scored 757 official goals during his playing days, Ronaldo and Messi have crossed the 700goal mark, and are still active in soccer as of 2021; Michael Schumacher and Lewis Hamilton stand out in Motorsports; Michael Phelps is a legend at swimming, he won a record of 28 medals in the Olympics, and has an all-time record of most gold medals by an individual, 23 gold medals across five summer Olympics; The late Mohammed Ali is arguably the greatest boxer of all time—he is the first boxer to win the world heavyweight championship for a record three times.

Sports could bring anyone into the limelight quickly, but it can also throw you out early as well. Getting out of sports could happen through injury, suspension for doping, or the star's inability to pay the required price—discipline. In basketball, injury cut short Yao Ming's, the Chinese-born former Houston Rockets center, career; in soccer, Owen Hargreaves, the former Manchester United midfielder's career was blighted by injuries that led to his early retirement; and in 1988, Jamaican-born Canadian sprinter, Ben Johnson, was stripped of his medals following the indictment of doping after winning a record-breaking gold medal in 100 meters sprint in 1988 Seoul Olympics.

Discipline is an important factor in sports. It is easier to remain disciplined when one is not yet in the limelight; it is not that facile after becoming famous. Several factors work against a sports star: money, attention from the opposite sex, parties, the press, hangers-on, a false sense of invincibility, and the demand from sponsors to attend events. Amidst the attention and demands on the star, in no time, he forgets what got him up there—hard work. On June 1, 2019, Andy Ruiz claimed the WBA (super), IBF, WBO, and IBO heavyweight titles from Anthony Joshua in one of the world's biggest upsets in boxing. On December 7, the same year, Andy lost all belts back to Joshua. Admittedly, he got carried away by the sudden fame and did not train adequately for the rematch despite several warnings from his trainers.

One of the unique characteristics of sports is that the legacy is not transferable; instead, standards are set for others to emulate and beat. When Pele retired in 1977, he had scored 767 official goals (Although, little known Josef Bican reportedly scored more goals; the Czechoslovakia history and statistics committee put it at 821 official goals). It took 44 years for Pele's record to be beaten by Ronaldo, and now, Messi is in the race to beat that same record. Legacy in sports is about setting standards and breaking records.

Music, Writing, and Arts

Music, writing, and the arts are specialized areas requiring natural talent and time to hone the skills. One of the most successful rock groups of the 20th century, the Beatles, started as teenagers from a High School band, the Quarrymen, which John Lennon formed in Liverpool in the 1950s. The group comprises the quartet of John Lennon, Paul McCartney, George Harrison, and Rugo Starr.

The Beatles' music went beyond England, becoming a global phenomenon. They were the best music selling act of all time; they sold about 600 million. They won several international awards: seven Grammy Awards, four Brit Awards, an Academy Award, and fifteen Ivor Novello Awards. They topped the charts for unprecedented times: the UK Albums Chart (fifteen) and Billboard Hot 100 chart (twenty). It was never in John Lennon's wildest dream that the band, which he started as a high school music group that played from club to club, would blossom to become legends in the music industry.

Other music artists and groups that left lasting legacies in the music industry are Elvis Presley, the Eagles, the Rolling Stones, Jimi Hendrix, James Brown, Bob Marley, Michael Jackson, Stevie Wonder, Whitney Houston, and Marvin Gaye.

Writing is another excellent opportunity to leave a legacy. One could do fictional (based on the writer's imagination) or non-fictional (writing based on the truth and accurate account of events, information, or people) books.

There are several genres of books; a few include Drama, Spirituality, Self-help, Motivation, Politics, Personal Development, Travel, Humor, and Crime.

Over the years, several authors have written classic books that propelled them to a legacy status: George Orwell (Animal Farm),

Charles Dickens (Oliver Twist), Napoleon Hill (Think and Grow Rich), William Shakespeare (Several plays), and Robert Kiyosaki (Rich Dad Poor Dad).

Customarily, you need the flair, command of the language, and good content to be a successful writer, but lately, the industry has mutated. There are now ghostwriters who can bring your literary idea to reality for a fee; online book sales platforms where an author can upload his work, and it will be on the shelves almost immediately; Print On Demand (POD), where printing is now based on customers' requests; and independent authorship—a writer does not need to go through the hurdle of a book agent before being accepted by a publisher/book sales platform.

Leonardo Da Vinci was an Italian-born, fifteenth-century painter, sculptor, architect, engineer, scientist, and theorist. However, he was famous for his paintings; Leonardo was regarded globally as one of the greatest painters that ever lived. His famous artworks are Mona Lisa, the last super, Vitruvian man, the virgin of the rocks, head of a woman, lady with ermine, savior of the world, and the portrait of Ginevra de Benci.

Other legendary artists are Michelangelo, Rembrandt, Vermeer, Jean-Antoine Watteau, Eugene Delacroix, Claude Monet, and Georges Seurat.

Power/Politics

Political officeholders have one of the best opportunities to leave lasting legacies; sadly, they seldom do. I recommend that political officeholders strive to achieve it; their actions have far-reaching implications on the nations they served. The impact of a politician's actions cuts across the nation's economy, interactions between the ethnic groups and political parties, international relations, infrastructural development, health care delivery, and educational standards. A political officeholder should not exchange the opportunity to leave a legacy for personal gains no matter the attractiveness. A political officeholder should be ready to forgo personal comfort for the greater good of the country; true leadership demands sacrifice.

Often, the political officeholder comes in with the best intentions but somehow, gets derailed. There is a plethora of factors that work against the officeholder; I will address a few of them below:

- Pressure from kingmakers
- Incompetent advisers
- False sense of entitlement and importance
- Fear of the unknown and possible future irrelevance.

Pressure from kingmakers happens more in democratic settings where there are agreements before elections with the power brokers for the political officeholder to act in a certain manner or protect particular interests. The existence of such an agreement will likely compromise the political officeholder's performance; he would have been structured to act in specific ways that could work against his legacy.

A political officeholder is as good as his advisers because he may not have complete knowledge of all the areas of governance. Political considerations may influence an officeholder to accept certain advisers instead of merit; where it occurs, he is likely on the path of a negative legacy.

In a false sense of entitlement, the political officeholder feels entitled to continue in office. It could result from a false sense of importance; the political officeholder thinks that he is the one with the knowledge and experience to solve the country's challenges. Megalomania is the extreme end of a false sense of entitlement; several incumbents exhibit this trait. No matter how good a political officeholder might be, the moment he plans to perpetuate himself in office, that is the beginning of the destruction of his positive legacies. Perpetuation in the office leads to dissent and agitations; the result is never pleasant.

Some political officeholders are afraid of life after office; they find it challenging to give up power as stipulated in the constitution or as promised on the assumption of office. The reality is that a political officeholder that left a positive legacy will continue to be relevant both in his country and international circles. On the exit from office, he becomes an elder statesman. Opportunities exist to counsel incumbents—both locally and internationally. He could be called upon to mediate in conflicts within and between nations, especially if he left a legacy in that area of governance. Former political officeholders also can deliver lectures for appreciable fees; the world has a lot to learn from their experience.

Many political officeholders are oblivious of the enormous opportunities that await them when their tenure expires. Some officeholders continue to adjust the constitution to perpetuate themselves in office. Another vital factor they do not consider is that their office is highly demanding on their time and health; they preside over meetings for long hours, read large volumes of reports, and make tough decisions. Despite their workloads, social engagements and travels equally need their attention. Suppose they leave office as when due, positive legacy beckons, and the control of their time; this will enable them to focus on other matters of interest. Perpetuation in the office is a ticket to leaving a negative legacy and a life of continuous stress.

The President of a country carries the country's burden. On Monday, April 19, 2021, shortly after the jury found Derek Chauvin guilty of the murder of George Floyd, the President of the United States, Joe Biden and his Vice, Kamala Harris, made a collective call to George Floyd's family to show their support. This act stresses the level of responsibility that accompanies such officeholders; they are expected to follow proceedings of events in different parts of the country and the world. The proceedings often require prompt and appropriate actions.

Humanity/Philanthropy

Humanity/philanthropy involves giving your resources and, or your time and energy for the good of others. Frequently, it is the use of one's surplus resources, but a few people have dedicated their lives to humanity as well. Several American industrialists in the 19th up till the 21st centuries have been at the forefront of philanthropy: Andrew Carnegie, John D. Rockefeller, Howard Hughes, Paul Allen, Mackenzie Scott, George Soros, Bill Gates, Warren Buffet, and Mike Bloomberg. They have set aside substantial resources and sometimes all their resources for philanthropy. Mother Teresa dedicated her life to helping the unloved and dying in India; she later extended it worldwide.

Philanthropy is an area one can affect lives beyond the immediate environment; structures exist that could enable one to carry out these activities without being physically involved. There are several foundations with clearly stated objectives of their areas of interest. One is at liberty to either set up a foundation or support existing foundations whose causes align with your interest. You can focus your philanthropist activities in several areas: education, research, health, sports, spirituality, infrastructure, and agriculture.

The general thinking is that only the wealthy can be involved in philanthropist activities; frequently, it is. However, one can still be involved through volunteer activities such as offering your time and experience in any cause of interest.

Philanthropy supports and compliments government efforts to provide infrastructure, education, and medical intervention. Most of the libraries in the United States, various Ivy League Universities, the eradication of some diseases, the development of some vaccines and cures, and specific knowledge available to humankind were all enabled by philanthropy. Philanthropy has indeed made the world a better place.

More billionaires worldwide have realized the importance of

philanthropy; they have taken appropriate steps by setting aside substantial resources to fund philanthropist activities through the *Giving Pledge*. The *Giving Pledge* is an initiative of Bill and Melinda Gates and Warren Buffett. Other philanthropy opportunities are setting up foundations and direct endowments.

Another outstanding characteristic of philanthropy is that boundaries do not limit it. An American philanthropist can be interested in eradicating mosquitoes in Africa; he does not need to come to Africa. The philanthropist can look for a credible research institute or foundation with similar interests and fund them. Malaria is currently the greatest killer in Africa. According to World Health Organization, malaria accounted for the death of over 409,000 Africans in 2019. If we extrapolate that figure, it means that malaria would have killed over 4 million people in Africa in the past decade. That figure equates to war and accidental deaths combined. The malaria parasite comes into the human body through the bite of an infected female Anopheles mosquito. Imagine a philanthropist funding the research that would eradicate mosquitoes in Africa; if that research is successful, such a legacy is almost indelible.

7 HOW TO IDENTIFY WHERE TO LEAVE A LEGACY

"If you would not be forgotten as soon as you are dead, either write something worth reading or do something worth writing."

……..Benjamin Franklin

The cliché' *leave a legacy* is often in use, but not many people get to leave a positive legacy behind. Not leaving a legacy is not always deliberate; often, it results from not having the consciousness and the know-how to take advantage of positive legacy opportunities. This chapter aims to bring us to speed on identifying positive legacy opportunities.

The development of positive legacy consciousness coupled with the knowledge of the different legacy areas should generate the desire to leave at least one positive legacy behind.

Knowing the different areas of legacy and understanding the distinction between foundational and non-foundational legacies have allowed everyone to know areas of legacy to focus. No matter how little endowed one is, one can work on any of the five identified foundational legacies: character, integrity, network/relationships, health, and spirituality.

Foundational legacy areas

After identifying the foundational legacies as fundamental, you need to strive to acquire them, taking into cognizance the areas that are easily accessible, or are of interest to you. Each of the foundational legacy areas has its uniqueness, and their nurturing processes differ. For instance, the skillset and effort needed in developing and nurturing networks/relationships are not the same as health or spirituality. Some may vary in requirement up to the point of countering each other. A monk that wants to develop his spirituality might need to withdraw into solitude for a period and do lots of meditation. The meditation process negates building networks/relationships. I suggest the pairing of legacy areas that the nurturing processes are compatible. Possible pairings are health/spirituality and character/network/relationships; this way, one can develop more than one legacy area at the same time while carrying out related activities.

Non-foundational legacy areas

Non-foundational legacies are not easily achievable by everyone; innate abilities, opportunities, and circumstances drive them. Sports is an activity that is accessible to all, but not everyone excels in them. If you excel in one, you may not excel in others even if they appear related. The current world record holder in 100 meters men's sprint as of 2021, Usain Bolt, toyed with the idea of playing soccer. He chose the forward position that needs a super-fast player to excel. One would expect

Usain Bolt to make a good forward in soccer—he failed. On retirement from basketball in 1993, Michael Jordan signed a contract with Minor League Baseball, the Chicago White Sox, in 1994—he had limited success. Marion Jones ruled track and field events in the late nineties, but the awarding organizations stripped her of most of her medals following her involvement in a drug scandal. On Marion Jones's return from prison, she tried her hand at basketball—she averaged one point per game and bowed out. The instances above amplify the reality that one cannot excel in all legacy areas, even within sports. In any legacy area, you need to identify your specific area of advantage and develop the skills; it is usually easier when you are young.

Stages in non-foundational legacy development

Below are suggested stages in non-foundational legacy development that should help you to leave a legacy in any area of interest.

- Identify your innate abilities
- Analyze the opportunities to excel and position yourself
- Pay the price
- Desire

Everyone is born with at least one ability; there are some things one does with ease, while others struggle with them. In college, there are some courses you excelled in with minimal effort, while you struggled to make the required grade in other courses after dissipating so much energy studying. In soccer, there are four basic positions: goalkeeping, defense, midfield, and attack. Coaches usually position players where they are best suited after considering their unique skills and physique. Coaches will typically not place a short person as a goalkeeper or defender; such persons are better suited for midfield and attack.

After identifying your innate abilities, you need to determine whether the opportunities exist to excel in your chosen field; non-exposure to opportunities has wasted many budding talents. In whichever area you want to excel in, the platform should exist to nurture and bring your innate abilities to the level of excellence and recognition. You cannot be a great writer with no form of education, and neither can you be a great cyclist without a cycling bicycle or cycling championships in your locality. Lionel Messi was a raw soccer talent in Argentina; his parents had to move to Barcelona to hone his soccer skills. Barcelona football club enrolled Messi in *La Masia*, the club's soccer academy; that singular act made Messi the legend that he has become.

The price for success is hard work and discipline; one needs the discipline to get to the top. Many talents have lost the opportunity to be legends in their chosen careers because of indiscipline. Some raw talents never got to the pinnacle of their careers because they could not cope with the rigors and demands of their profession. There is no shortcut to success; while some schools of thought are coming up with the idea of smart work, it does not precede hard work. The person who has worked hard eventually finds a way to do it better and faster; that process in my opinion, is smart work.

Talent, discipline, and hard work will get you up there, but you need the desire to remain on top. Often, many talents fall off the cliff because they lose the desire to continue to pay the price shortly after achieving success. Recall that I told Andy Ruiz's story earlier; he only held the belts for six months—Andy lacked the desire.

Other factors

Aside from the above-stated stages in developing non-foundational legacies, other factors could influence where to leave a legacy:

- Personality
- Association
- Resources
- Life's experiences

We are all wired differently; even siblings exposed to the same circumstances and conditions think and act distinctively. Mother Teresa was not the only one in the Sisters of Loreto; neither was she the only one that saw the sick, the poor, and the unloved in the slums of Calcutta in India. Also, it is not only India that has slums with an army of the sick, poor, unloved, and dying; but it took innate desire, compassionate **personality**, self-belief, and determination to put her career on the line for an uncharted cause. Recall that she had little or no resources when she started, no support from anyone, and was single without a family in India. All she possessed was compassion, desire, and resolve. Another attribute of Mother Teresa's personality was self-belief. What she started in 1950 was unprecedented; convincing the convent hierarchy to approve her withdrawal for an unproven cause and the Calcutta city officials to allow her to use an abandoned building are pieces of evidence of her personality. Many may have thought of helping the sick and dying in several countries, but obvious obstacles could have put paid to such desires. Perhaps, Mother Teresa's compassionate nature was a product of her mother's influence—that is correct—but she is the youngest of three siblings and appears to be the only one that took the mother's tutelage to global recognition.

Many of our actions are traceable to our *associations;* they influence how we behave, especially those we look up to or that have earned our respect. Sometimes, the association may not be direct, but if you agree with a person's ideology, especially when it is documented, you indirectly associate with the person. Scottish-born American steel magnate, Andrew Carnegie, was not just a successful business owner; he was also an avid reader and an excellent writer. He contributed several articles in the popular newspapers of his time and wrote several books where he shared his thoughts on several topics, particularly on wealth management. The compilation of his articles on surplus wealth management birthed the thought-provoking book, *The gospel of Wealth.* In the book, he questioned the traditional bequest system of passing on all surplus wealth to one's dependents. Carnegie suggested the management of surplus assets by the wealthy during **their** lifetime for the greater good of humankind and society. John D. Rockefeller was an industrialist that redefined oil production, refining, and distribution in the United States and globally between the nineteenth and twentieth centuries. Andrew Carnegie and John D. Rockefeller were somewhat contemporaries; while Carnegie ruled the Steel world, Rockefeller held sway in the oil industry. Both were competitors at some point; they ventured into each other's areas of business. During my inquiry, I did not come across any documented material that showed direct interaction between Carnegie and Rockefeller; nonetheless, it appears that Carnegie may have influenced Rockefeller through his writings. Rockefeller's post-retirement activities allude to that fact as it aligns with Carnegie's ideology. The ideas Carnegie put forward regarding wealth management then were unprecedented.

Resources at one's disposal could determine where one can leave legacies. It takes enormous resources to focus on some specific causes. Rockefeller almost single-handedly established the University of Chicago. Andrew Carnegie started setting up libraries in the United States and worldwide; he reportedly developed over 2,800 libraries in his lifetime. Mother Teresa taught us that finance is not the only resource that one needs for philanthropy; attitude, skills, and time are resources available to pursue specific causes. Before Mother Teresa started her mission, she already had skills and experience in education management but lacked medical skills. She went to Holy Family Hospital in Patna, India, to acquire the basic skills in medicine; she must have known that she would need both medicine and education management knowledge to pursue her cause successfully.

Life's experiences play a significant role in determining the areas to leave legacies; several were born out of these experiences. Andrew

Carnegie's parents' relocation from Scotland to the United States in 1848, when Carnegie was 12 years old, was supposed to have put paid to his education. Carnegie went to work immediately with Anchor Cotton Mills, a 12 hour a day, six days of a week job for $1.2/week. A job he described as highly stressful for a boy of his age. However, he was able to educate himself through the benevolence of Col. James Anderson, a local business owner in Allegheny, Pennsylvania; he opened his private library for young working-class men's use. His kind gesture enabled Carnegie to fulfill his potential in education. The singular gesture from Col. Anderson would have informed Carnegie's decision to build public libraries as one of his core areas of philanthropy. The first public library Carnegie funded was in Allegheny, Pennsylvania, and in front of the building is a sculpture to honor Col. James Anderson. At the top of the statue is the burst of Col. Anderson, and beneath it is a young workman reading—the sculpture tells the story.

Alfred Nobel's discovery of dynamite and making a fortune out of it was a typical success story until he read his supposed obituary while still alive. Ludvig, Alfred's older brother, died in Cannes, France and a tabloid mistook Ludvig for Alfred by publishing an uncomplimentary remark, *"The Merchant of Death is Dead."* The experience most likely informed the change of Alfred's will; he set up an endowment fund for the Nobel Prize—one of the world's prestigious awards.

8 LEGACY AND VISION

"Create the highest grandest vision possible for your life, because you become what you believe."

.......*Oprah Winfrey*

A vision is an audacious mental picture of a future possibility for oneself, organization, country, continent, or the world. The vision should be clear and compelling enough to stimulate continued action towards its achievement. Vision is futuristic; it articulates a possible achievement in a specified medium to long-term period, usually five years and over. It specifies where you are going, why you are going, and when you intend to get there.

In answering the why question, vision defines and clarifies the purpose, implying that the vision tells where it is headed and states the reason for going in that direction. You may not know which route to follow at the point of visioning, whether you are going by rail, car, walking, flying, or boat. One thing is sure, you are going there, and you know why you want to get there.

The clarity of thought of where you are headed, and the purpose and the time frame will help you decide the most appropriate plan to achieve your envisioned targets. The plan shows the best route that enables the achievement of the imagined objective.

The characteristics of a vision statement are listed below:

- Futuristic
- Ambitious
- Clarity
- Compelling
- Imaginative.

Visions are stated in future terms, and it is usually on a medium to long-term basis, five years and above. The stated achievement period calls the visioner to action.

Targets in visions are usually ambitious. They may appear unrealistic to outsiders because at the time of visioning, very few or likely nobody is convinced that the visioner can achieve the feat.

Clarity and unambiguity are among the attributes of visions; this attribute requires that the vision be stated in measurable terms. For example, achieving $100million in sales revenue from this book or expressed in the superlative form, *this book will be one of the best-sellers in the 21st century.*

The vision should be compelling enough to galvanize the visioner and the team to action; there should be enough enthusiasm to keep them going despite the obstacles they may encounter.

Although the vision is clear, it is an imagination that is so palpable that the visioner can communicate it lucidly enough for others to understand and buy into it.

I will explore below two great visioners of the 21st century: Bill Gates and Elon Musk. We will see how their audacious visions have come to reality, thereby culminating in a legacy.

Bill Gates

Born William Henry Gates III, on October 28, 1955, in Seattle, Washington, United States, he co-founded Microsoft Corporation, the world's largest personal computer software company with Paul Allen.

Gates foray into computing started in his high school, Lakeside School, Washington, where he met his longtime friend and associate, Paul Allen. Lakeside School Mother's Club bought computing time in a Teletype Model 33 computer for the students' use. Gates, Allen, and two other pupils were so enthralled by the wonder machine that they took advantage of a bug in it to schedule additional time for themselves. The involved quartet got caught, and they were suspended from using the machine for a period. Gates learned how to code early; he developed a payroll and class scheduling system for the school. He used the class scheduling system to his advantage by scheduling himself amongst girls. Gates later formed a company with Paul, Traf-O-Data; the company developed a computer program that analyzed traffic information in the city. They sold the program to the city council officials.

In 1973, Gates enrolled in Harvard for a pre-law major in line with his father's wishes but took mathematics and computing courses at the graduate level. Gates met Steve Ballmer, who later became the CEO of Microsoft in Harvard.

In 1975, Gates and Allen sold the idea of a BASIC interpreter to Micro Instrumentation and Telemetry Systems (MITS) for their Altair 8800 computer. MITS engaged Paul; Gates dropped out of Harvard to join Paul in MITS, and they formed Microsoft.

Following a recommendation by Gates's mum, IBM engaged

Microsoft to develop an interpreter for their newly created personal computer. Microsoft made a deal with Seattle Computer Products (SCP), adapted its 86-DOS, and delivered it to IBM as PC DOS (Personal Computer Disc Operating System) for a one-time fee of $50,000. Since there was no exclusivity agreement with IBM, Microsoft designed another version for other personal computer manufacturers as MS-DOS (Microsoft Disc Operating System). The development of Windows in 1995 was a response to Apple's Macintosh GUI; GUI was more user-friendly than MS-DOS. As of 2021, Microsoft Windows controls about 75% of the operating systems market globally.

The Vision of Microsoft

Bill Gates and Paul Allen had a clear vision of where Microsoft was headed when they formed the company in 1975. In Gates's words, on the company's 40th anniversary in 2015, he stated,

"Early on, Paul Allen and I set a goal of a computer on every desk in every home. It was a bold idea, and a lot of people thought that we were out of our minds to imagine it as possible."

Gates further stated,

"It is amazing to think about how far computing has come since then, and we can all be proud of the role Microsoft played in that revolution."

The first statement is a vision statement. If we subject it to the characteristics of a vision statement earlier discussed, you will see that it virtually met them. The statement was futuristic as of when they set out. The only difference was that they did not put a time frame to achieving their objective. Computers back then were mainly mainframes housed in vast rooms—they were quite big. How the gigantic computers could be contained within a desk was then unthinkable—that was ambitious at that time. However, their aim was clear: the mainframe must be miniaturized to fit into people's desks.

The idea was mind-blowing and compelling; it could only be possible in Gates and Allen's imagination.

It is ironic that all the personal computers found on people's desks, as envisioned by Gates and Allen, do not bear Microsoft; they bear Compaq in those early days and in current times, Dell, HP, Apple, Toshiba, and Sony. However, 75% of the operating system that runs on the computers is Microsoft Windows as of 2021. Microsoft has a more considerable market value than any individual personal computer maker. Little wonder that Bill Gates, the highest shareholder in Microsoft, was the richest man in the world for nearly two decades, spanning 1995 to 2017, with cameos by Warren Buffett in 2008 and Carlos Slim Helu and his family (2010–2013). Jeff Bezos of Amazon took over the top spot in 2018 and remained there up to 2021, while Elon Musk continues to breathe down his neck to take the top spot.

Bill Gates and Paul Allen's vision to put a personal computer on the desk of every home has put them in a legacy position. Providence nevertheless placed Bill Gates as the root legacy. Bill Gates's root legacy status does not diminish Paul Allen's contribution; Paul bowed to the cold hands of death on October 15, 2018.

Elon Musk

Elon Reeve Musk was born on June 28, 1971, in Pretoria, South Africa, to a Canadian mother that was raised in South Africa and a South African Father. Musk developed an interest in computers at the age of 10 years; at 12 years, he taught himself how to write codes using manuals and created a video game which he sold to a magazine in South Africa for $500.

After a brief stint at the University of Pretoria, South Africa, Musk took advantage of his maternal roots to get Canadian citizenship, and he relocated in June 1989. On arrival in Canada, he enrolled in Queens University in Kingston, Ontario. Two years later, Musk transferred to the University of Pennsylvania, United States; he graduated with two bachelor's degrees: Physics and Economics in 1997. Having spent only two days at Stanford University for his Ph.D., Musk dropped out of the program to get a slice of the internet boom.

He partnered with his brother Kimbal Musk to form Zip2, an online magazine directory. They sold it to Compaq for $307million in 1999. Now cash-rich, Elon and Kimbal founded an online payment platform, X.com, in 1999. X.com later merged with Confinity in 2000 and renamed the service Paypal in 2001. eBay acquired Paypal in 2002 for $1.5billion; Elon got $180million from the sale of Paypal.

Elon Musk's visions

Elon Musk is multi-visionary; I will attempt to capture his visions in his four (maybe six) principal endeavors and let us see how he has fared.

- In his tweet on March 21, 2021, *"I am accumulating resources to help make life multi-planetary and extend the light of consciousness to the stars."* I assume this to be SpaceX's vision.

- Tesla's vision statement is *"To create the most compelling car company of the 21st century by driving the world's transition to electric vehicles."*

- The Boring Company's vision statement is to *"Build a large network of fast-to-dig, low-cost tunnels to help alleviate congestion and enable rapid transit across densely populated regions."*

- Neuralink's vision is *"to connect the human brain to artificial intelligence for medical purposes."*

Elon Musk formed SpaceX in 2002 with two primary objectives:

i)   To provide a cheaper alternative to space travel
ii) To colonize the red planet—Mars.

In 2017, Elon Musk presented a design for Big Falcon Rocket that can carry a minimum of 100 people to Mars; he also revealed a target achievement date of 2022.

In 2020, *SpaceX* was the first privately owned American company to successfully send four astronauts to the international space station from American soil through the Dragon capsule. Between 2011 and 2020, the United States transported its astronauts through the Russian space crafts after retiring their space shuttle in 2011.

SpaceX has largely achieved the first objective, and it appears to be on course in achieving its long-term vision—making the world multi-planetary. Going by the contracts that United States' NASA (National Aeronautics and Space Administration) has given to SpaceX so far, the International Space Station shuttle appears to be a dress rehearsal for the long-term vision.

The distance from the earth to the International Space Station (ISS) is 408 kilometers, while the distance from the earth to the shortest distance to Mars is 55 million kilometers. It takes about 6hrs to get to ISS, while it takes 6-8 months to get to Mars (with the latest technology). Musk aims to achieve the feat of taking humans to Mars in 2022—the world is watching.

Tesla's vision to create the most compelling company in the 21st century is on track; all Tesla's cars are 100% electric with zero emissions (From the Roadster in 2009, Model S in 2012, Model X SUV in 2015, Model 3 Sedan in 2017, and Model Y Crossover in 2020). As of 2020, Tesla was the most valued car company with a total market capitalization peaking at $847billion in January 2021, from an obscure position of about 10% of the same value a year earlier.

The Boring Company is Elon Musk's vision to reduce commuting time and cost between major cities in the United States by developing the hyperloop as an alternative to the high-speed train; Musk expects it to be cheaper by 90% and faster by 500%. The current fasted train travels at 150 miles per hour; the hyperloop's target is to travel at 750miles per hour, almost the equivalent to the speed of sound (767 miles per hour). Musk envisions a 28passenger pneumatic tube traveling through a tunnel. The technology is still in its infancy; Musk's development strategy is to use external designers through competitions.

In May 2019, the Boring Company was awarded a contract by Las Vegas Convention to build an underground loop system to shuttle people around Las Vegas Convention Center. The success of the Las Vegas Convention project should boost the achievement of the Boring Company's vision.

Neuralink is an artificial intelligence company formed by Elon Musk in 2016. The idea behind the company is to insert a chip into the human brain that can read human thoughts; the chip communicates with the computer and programmable machines. Commands can be carried out by programmable equipment just by thinking about the tasks. The rationale behind the project is for medical reasons: to cure paralysis and neurological disorders, restore sensory and movement functions, and increase the communication channels with the brain. Although work has started by Neuralink on the project, the concept is yet to be proven practicable.

Aside from the four projects mentioned above, Elon Musk is also involved in two other projects: *Starlink* and *Solar City*. Starlink offers fast-speed broadband internet access to remote and urban areas through satellites from orbit. Starlink is taking advantage of opportunities that arose from SpaceX's foray into space technology; it has the ambition to generate up to $30billion in revenue in the short run. Starlink appears to compliment Elon Musk's vision of making the world multi-planetary by helping to raise funds to support the long-term vision of SpaceX. SpaceX's current customer is limited to United States' NASA. Musk co-founded Solar City with his cousins in 2006. Tesla acquired Solar City in 2016 and merged it with Tesla's battery storage division to form Tesla energy. Solar City can be viewed as aligning with Tesla's mission of providing clean energy.

Elon Musk's continued pursuance of his visions has brought him great fortune. As of March 2021, Musk was the second richest man globally; he was worth $156.9 billion, second only to Jeff Bezos of Amazon according to Bloomberg Billionaires Index. Musk was on different occasions the richest man in the world in 2021; he does not appear to want to back down as Tesla shares continue to soar in 2022.

Taking a cue from Oprah Winfrey's quote, creating a high and grand vision and pursuing it leaves you with one possible result—legacy status.

9 THE MAGNETIC FORCE IN LEGACY

Most of the world's challenges today are offshoots of some persons' legacies; consequently, we should be careful of the legacies we leave behind because our beliefs and lifestyles could positively or negatively influence others. Several terrorist attacks abound across the globe that sprouts from the influences of fanatics.

On December 21, 1988, Pan Am flight 103 was bombed with a total casualty of 270 people, including the passengers and crew; the legacy of this dastardly act was traced to Libyan authorities. On September 11, 2001, two aircraft rammed into the World Trade Centre, killing about 2,700 people in the World Trade Center alone and roughly another 300 in the other two aircraft; the legacy was traced to al-Qaeda. On July 7, 2005, a coordinated bombing in London killed 52 people of varying nationalities; this was linked to Islamist fundamentalists in London. Lastly, on June 12, 2016, terrorists linked to ISIL attacked a nightclub in

Orlando, United States, killing 49 people. Each of the attacks is a product of an ideology, the root legacy may have done the planning, but the execution is usually carried out by those they have influenced.

The challenge with negative influences is that they do not die with the originators, just as with positive influences. At the demise of the originator of the negative legacy, they usually leave behind protégées whom they have indoctrinated with the ideology. I will explore two classic instances: al-Qaeda and The North/South Korea quandary.

Al-Qaeda

Al-Qaeda is a word of Arabic origin, meaning *the base*. It was formed by Osama bin Laden, a Saudi-born Jihadist of Yemen descent. Osama bin Laden primarily created al-Qaeda to resist the occupation of Afghanistan by the Soviet Union in 1979. When the Soviets exited Afghanistan in 1989, the attention of al-Qaeda shifted to the United States' dominance of the Middle East. Osama bin Laden became critical of the Saudi royal family; he slipped into Sudan despite the Saudi authorities seizing his passport in 1991. In 1996, following United States' pressure on the Sudanese government, Osama bin Laden left Sudan for Afghanistan.

Al-Qaeda committed several terrorist acts against the United States between 1993 and 2001. Notably, the World Trade Center bombing of 1993 that killed six people and injured over 1,000; the combined embassies attacks of August 7, 1998, of Dar es Salaam, Tanzania, and Nairobi, Kenya, that killed 224 people; and the brazen attack on United States soil on September 11, 2001, where they used four commercial aircraft as weapons of attack. In the September 11 attack, also known as 9/11, 2996 people were killed—most of them from the Twin Towers of the World Trade Center.

Following the 9/11 attack, the United States government requested the extradition of Osama bin Laden from the Taliban government of Afghanistan; the refusal of the Taliban led to the invasion of Afghanistan by the United States on October 7, 2001. At year-end, the Taliban had lost almost all the territories aside from the rural areas forcing Osama bin Laden to go into hiding *(the United States troops withdrew from Afghanistan on August 30, 2021, and allowed the Taliban to regain control of the country).*

On May 2, 2011, barely ten years after the 9/11 attack, the United States Navy SEALs killed Osama bin Laden in his hideout in Abbottabad, Pakistan. The death of Osama bin Laden ended an era in al-Qaeda. Egyptian-born Ayman al-Zawahiri became the new emir of al-Qaeda six weeks later.

Although Osama bin Laden has died, his ideology nonetheless is still alive, al-Qaeda has become fragmented and decentralized, but they are still potent. For al-Qaeda to still be formidable after the death of Osama bin Laden means that he has successfully sold his ideas to his protégées.

North/South Korea quandary

Japan occupied Korea from 1910 to 1945. After the surrender of Japan in World War II in 1945, the Soviet Union and the United States divided the Korean peninsula into two zones along latitude 38°N, also known as the 38th parallel. The Soviet Union occupied the North, while the United States occupied the South. Kim Il-sung led the communist North, and Syngman Rhee held sway in the anti-communist South.

The Soviet Union withdrew from North Korea in 1948; the United States followed suit in the South in 1949. After their withdrawals, mistrust brewed between the North and the South. On suspicion of an invasion by the South, the North preemptively invaded the South on June 25, 1950. The United Nations Security Council supported the South, while China supported the North; they agreed to an armistice in 1953. Armistice implies that North and South Korea are still technically at war because they are yet to sign a peace treaty. The Korean war accounted for the death of approximately 3 million Koreans.

Kim II-sung was the leader of post-World War II North Korea; he instituted a dynasty of the Kims. Kim II-sung died in 1994, and his son Kim Jong-il took over from his father, Kim II-sung. Kim Jong-il continued the policy of absolutism, military first, and the theory of *Juche* instituted by his father. Kim Jong-il died in December 2011; his second son, Kim Jong-un, replaced him as the supreme leader.

The dynasty of the Kims' family in North Korea is now in its third generation. All the regimes essentially have the same ideologies but with slight variations. They retained the core policy of absolutism, military first, and *Juche*.

In *absolutism,* the supreme leader is all-powerful and does not accommodate opposition. Dissensions are decisively contained: close allies have been removed and some purportedly murdered for dissension offenses.

The *military first* policy has made North Korea have one of the largest armies worldwide in terms of personnel. They have continually pursued nuclear weapons development and constantly shown belligerence to their Southern neighbors. Their flagrant nuclear test continues to create tension in the region.

The *Juche* is a national ideology that is based on self-reliance as a basis for achieving true socialism. Unfortunately, North Koreans are yet to experience the positive impact of the ideology on their living standards.

From the examples above, we can see that protégées seldom deviate from the pattern of the ideologists. Therefore, the responsibility is on the ideologists to get it right from the outset. I advise that every advocate of a belief system should first subject that belief and related actions to the 7-way test, as enunciated in chapter 5, How to develop legacy consciousness. At a minimum, test 2—FAIR to All and test 7—Would it make the WORLD a BETTER PLACE? Irrespective of one's convictions and motivations, these tests should rank higher because they have a broader reach and implications than personal ambitions.

10 WEALTH OR HUMANITY, WHICH HAS A LONGER-LASTING LEGACY?

'Poor and restricted are our opportunities in this life; narrow our horizon; our best work most imperfect; but rich men should be thankful for one inestimable boon. They have it in their power during their lives to busy themselves in organizing benefactions from which the masses of their fellows will derive lasting advantage, and thus dignify their own lives."

.... Andrew Carnegie

While I was putting this book together, a question came to my mind, Wealth or Humanity, which has a longer-lasting legacy? As I pondered it, the exploits of four personalities came to my consciousness: Mansa Musa, Andrew Carnegie, John D. Rockefeller, and Mother Teresa. I will explore the legacies of these trailblazers regarding their wealth and philanthropist endeavors. Their achievements should help to address the question.

Mansa Musa (1280–1337)

Mansa Musa was born Kankan Musa; he ascended the throne of the Mali Empire in 1312 under a unique circumstance. Mansa Musa's predecessor, Mansa Abubakari, who ascended the throne in 1300, wanted to expand his influence beyond the Atlantic Ocean. He spared no cost to achieve the feat; in his first effort, he built a fleet of 200 boats fully loaded with victuals that would last the voyagers for several years. The Mansa instructed the chief admiral not to return until they had gotten to the Atlantic Ocean's end or when they exhausted their supplies; after several years—only one boat returned. The emperor questioned the boat captain, and he said that all the other boats ran into a whirlpool in the middle of the ocean and disappeared; only his boat turned back. Not giving up on his quest, the emperor prepared another fleet of 1000 boats and embarked on the journey under his command in 1311—the emperor never returned.

The practice in the Mali Empire then was that if the emperor was not physically present in the kingdom for a period, he usually appointed one of the potential heirs to deputize for him. Kankan Musa, the younger (half) brother of Mansa Abubakari, usually plays the role. After waiting for about a year for Emperor Abubakari, Kankan Musa became the Mansa (Emperor) in 1312. It is remarkable that despite the failure of Mansa Abubakari's expedition, his courage and ambition are applaudable.

The Mali Empire was one of the largest empires in the world in the 14th century. It covered about 1.25 million square kilometers and spanned part of the Ghana Empire, Guinea, Senegal, Southern Mauritania, Gambia, Guinea-Bissau, Ivory Coast, Northern Burkina Faso, and Western Niger.

Mansa Musa met a wealthy empire, and he expanded the empire's prosperity through conquests of land, commerce, arts and culture, education, and spirituality; nonetheless, he was famous for his prosperity. Mansa Musa was reputed to be the wealthiest man to have ever lived; he was estimated to be worth over $400billion in current terms. However, the argument in some quarters is that it is impossible to estimate his wealth in contemporary times. Mansa Musa accumulated wealth through salt, gold, and elephant ivory trade; the empire had these commodities in abundance.

Not much was known of Mansa Musa until 1324, when he embarked on the holy pilgrimage to Mecca; he traveled with an entourage of 60,000, including 12,000 slaves. All of them were well-dressed in brocades and Persian silk. He also went along with 100 elephants and 80 camels. The large procession carried enough victuals to cater to themselves for the year's journey spanning 4,300 kilometers. The estimate of gold he took along was over 20 tonnes. Mansa Musa was generous with the gold; he gave out gold bars to the poor as they traveled. The gold bars he gave out soon flooded the Egyptian gold market; prices of gold fell sharply in Cairo, Medina, and Mecca; it remained so for over ten years. Mansa Musa borrowed all the gold he could find from lenders to stabilize the market as he returned despite the high interest.

The show of splendor and kindness reverberated beyond Africa; it spread as far as Europe. Spanish-Jewish cartographer, Abraham Cresques, had to map Mali and depict Mansa Musa in the medieval map-work, the Catalan Atlas, in Majorca, an Island in Spain. Cresques published the Catalan Atlas in 1375. In the Atlas, Cresques portrayed Mansa Musa as a king, with a gold bar in one hand and a golden staff in the other; the depiction signifies royalty and splendor. The Catalan Atlas portrayal further popularized Mansa Musa and the Empire of Mali in Europe. The thinking in many quarters is that Mansa Musa's pilgrimage to Mecca in 1324 was more than a holy pilgrimage but an opportunity to announce Mali to the world.

Mansa Musa purportedly built a minimum of one mosque every week; he brought architects from Spain and Egypt to build his grand palace in Timbuktu. One of his enduring legacies is the Djinguereber Mosque in Timbuktu; it was commissioned in 1327 by Mansa Musa. The mosque is still standing up to the present time.

Mansa Musa reportedly died in 1337, at an estimated age of 56 years, after ruling the Mali Empire for 25 years. He left the Mali Empire economically strong with a vast knowledge base and significantly, the University of Sankore in Timbuktu, where he brought in the finest astronomers, jurists, and mathematicians. His son, Mansa Maghan, succeeded him in 1337.

Sadly, Timbuktu, which enjoyed so much attention in government presence, trade, education, and culture during Mansa Musa's reign in the 14th century, is a shadow of its old self. It is still in present-day Mali but has a population of a little over 55,000. As a result of several invasions and other factors: Touareg in the 15th century, Songhai in the 16th century, Moroccan army in the 16th century, and desertification, Timbuktu is now an impoverished town with little evidence of its glorious past. The trade routes for salt, gold, elephant ivory, scholars, and cultural edifices are gone. Over the years, Timbuktu might have lost its splendor; however, its place in history should still attract tourists that may want to have firsthand knowledge of Mansa Musa's lifestyle and the city's cultural and scholarly heritage. The activities of terrorists—al-Qaeda in the Islamic Maghreb in the Sahel region—has sounded a death knell to the possible tourism potential of Timbuktu.

Andrew Carnegie (1835–1919)

Andrew Carnegie is a Scottish-born American industrialist who made his fortune in the steel industry; he is often referred to as the father of modern philanthropy. Following the challenging times his father's handloom profession faced in Scotland, the family migrated to the United States when he was 12 years old. New technologies arose in the cotton processing industry that phased out the manual handloom weaving process. Carnegie senior felt America presented the opportunity for a better life; he disposed of all his assets in Dunfermline, Scotland, and headed to the United States, where he had relatives that had already settled.

On arrival in Allegheny, Pennsylvania, father and son got employment with a Scottish-owned cotton mill, Anchor Cotton Mills; young Carnegie started as a bobbin boy at $1.2 per week. Andrew Carnegie's coming to America was supposed to scuttle his formal education, but that did not deter him from educating himself. He took advantage of every opportunity, including night schooling, to get educated. A year after arriving at Allegheny, he got employed as a telegraph messenger boy in the Pittsburgh office of the Ohio Telegraph company with the help of an uncle.

Carnegie met his mentor, Thomas Scott, in the telegraph company. When he was 18 years, Thomas Scott employed him as a secretary/telegraph operator for Pennsylvania Railroad Company. A combination of hard work, quick learning, attention to detail, and continuous education endeared Carnegie to Thomas Scott; Scott offered him a higher position as the Superintendent of the Western Division of the Railroad Company.

Carnegie's foray into investment was through his benefactor, Thomas Scott, who used his relationship with Adams Express company to help Carnegie make his first investment; Carnegie purchased ten shares in Adams Express Company. The investment started yielding dividends immediately. Carnegie later invested in other businesses, particularly the Sleeping Car company, founded by Theodore Woodruff: he acquired it later. In his early thirties, Carnegie quit his paid employment and formed the Iron Bridge Building Company and a Telegraph company. He continued to do business with the Pennsylvania Railroad Company, and in a short while, Carnegie became a wealthy man.

The discovery and patenting of the Bessemer process, a pneumatic-based steel production process by the British inventor Henry Bessemer, in 1856, paved the way for Carnegie to become the world's biggest steel manufacturer. The Bessemer process is a steel production technique that replaced the heat-based crucible process that had been in operation since 1751—the Bessemer process was cheaper and faster.

In partnership with some associates, Carnegie formed Carnegie, McCandless, and Company. The company constructed Edgar Thomson

Steel Works, named after the then-president of Pennsylvania Railroad: a strategic move to court the patronage of the Pennsylvania Railroad. Carnegie and his partners built or acquired other steel plants, especially the open-hearth furnace plant in Homestead, Pennsylvania. In 1892, Carnegie incorporated the Carnegie Steel Company to merge all the various steel plants the company had owned. Through an adept combination of efficient management of resources, acquisition, and control of raw materials, Carnegie Steel Company achieved a good return on investment of roughly 40%, which enabled it to become the biggest steel company globally.

In 1901, J.S. Morgan bought Carnegie Steel Company through his company, United States Steel Corporation, for $480million in exchange for a 5% 50-year-old bond; $230million worth of the shares belonged to Carnegie. There was no exchange of immediate cash in the transaction: only a promise of future payment.

After the sale of Carnegie Steel Company, Carnegie shifted his attention to philanthropy and writing. He gave out about $350million of his fortune during his lifetime. Carnegie was a product of libraries; he educated himself through private studies. Although the actual number is in dispute, several reports suggest that Carnegie funded the construction of over 2,800 libraries worldwide during his lifetime. Carnegie's other philanthropic gestures include the donation of about 8,000 organs to different churches, the founding of the Carnegie Foundation, the funding of the Carnegie Institute of Science, Carnegie Mellon University, and several other causes such as research in science, education, world peace, and arts.

Carnegie loved books and writing; he befriended famous writers and published several essays, articles, and books. One of his famous essays turned book, *the gospel of wealth*, was written in 1889. In the book, Carnegie asserts that the man of wealth has a duty to society by using his superior experience for the greater good of humankind. Carnegie further stated that the man of wealth has responsibilities: he should live a simple life and avoid extravagance, provide enough for his dependents, and use the surplus for the greater good of humankind. He made a controversial comment, *"The man who dies thus rich dies disgraced."* Carnegie strongly disagrees with the traditional manner of bequeathing wealth to heirs that he believes are often not equipped to manage it. He supported the British heavy taxation system on the estate left behind by the dead. Carnegie believes that one's life should be shared into three parts: the first part to focus on getting as much education as possible; the second, to make as much money as possible; and the third, to use the resources to pursue worthwhile causes.

Carnegie was a dedicated family man and somewhat enigmatic; he lived as a bachelor with his mother until she died in 1886. At 51 years of age, he married a lady 20 years his junior, Louise Whitfield; they had a daughter, Margaret.

John D. Rockefeller (1839–1937)

John D. Rockefeller was of humble beginnings. He became one of the wealthiest men in the world through a combination of foresight, hard work, perseverance, astuteness, and some good fortune. At the height of his wealth, he amassed over $400billion in current times.

John was the second child, born in a family of six children, in Richford, New York, to parents with contrasting character traits. His mother, Eliza Davison, was a strict and devout Christian of the Baptist denomination, while his father, William Avery 'Bill' Rockefeller, was an easy-going man and described in some quarters as a con artist. At 12 years, Rockefeller had saved up $50 ($1,400 in current times) from selling candies, potatoes, and raising turkeys; he lent out the money to a local farmer at 7% interest. The deal taught him to see money as a tool to serve him rather than working for it. When he was 14 years old, the family moved to Strongsville, a suburb of Cleveland, Ohio.

After completing high school at 16 years, Rockefeller attended a 10week course in bookkeeping in Folsom's commercial college, Cleveland. He was employed by Hewitt and Tuttle, a merchandising and produce brokerage firm. Four years later, at 20 years, Rockefeller and Maurice B. Clark put $4,000 together, mainly from a bank loan, formed a partnership, and started a merchandising and brokerage business in agricultural products. They specialized in grains, hay, meat, and other related products. Barely a year after the start of the partnership, they had generated $450,000 ($12.6million in current terms) in revenue.

Rockefeller got incongruent parental influences: dishonesty and ruthlessness from his father, but faith, diligence, self-control, and thriftiness from his mother. Rockefeller senior admitted to a neighbor that he deliberately cheated his children in dealings with them to sharpen their business acumen; this may have influenced his business dealings.

In 1859, George Bissell and Edwin Drake successfully drilled oil using rig technology near Titusville, Pennsylvania. In 1863, in partnership with Maurice B. Clark and Samuel Andrews, Rockefeller established the first oil refinery in Cleveland. Soon, they became significant players in the region. The initial success made him focus his attention on the oil business: refining kerosine—the commodity of choice for lighting up homes in that era.

In 1870, Rockefeller established Standard Oil in partnership with William Rockefeller, Samuel Andrews, Stephen Harkness, and Henry Flagler. Rockefeller had bought out Maurice Clark in 1865 from the earlier partnership.

Various factors such as mergers and acquisitions, competition elimination, favorable railroad rebates, and other favorable economic conditions enhanced Standard oil's rapid growth. Standard oil also ventured into the transportation of its oil through deals with railway companies, the purchase of existing pipelines and terminals, and the construction of new ones.

Standard oil bought out competitors, and in less than ten years, it became a monopoly in the United States. It controlled oil wells, transportation, and distribution. At its peak, Standard oil accounted for over 90% of America's drilling, refining, transportation, and marketing capacity. It oversaw 20,000 oil wells, 6,500 kilometers of pipelines, and over 5,000 tank cars. The size of Standard oil became an issue in the United States despite its effort to reorganize the company into independently run organizations. The success of Standard oil exposed Rockefeller to muckraking journalists, especially those affected by his many business conquests. In 1911, the United States supreme court found Standard Oil to have violated the Sherman Antitrust Act and broke Standard oil into 34 independently run companies. Among them are ExxonMobil, British Petroleum, ConocoPhillips, Chevron, and many others. Most of the companies are still operating in different names following mergers and acquisitions.

The breaking down of Standard oil into separately run entities was a blessing in disguise to Rockefeller. Each entity grew rapidly; the sum of the different parts became much more than the whole. Since Rockefeller held substantial stakes in all the entities, it propelled him to become supremely rich.

In 1897, at 58 years, Rockefeller retired quite early from the day-to-day running of his vast empire and focused on philanthropy. Rockefeller and the American Baptist Education Society combined to provide the initial endowment funds of $600,000 to start Chicago University—Rockefeller gave over $80million to the University during his lifetime. Rockefeller admitted that supporting the University of Chicago was the best investment he ever made. He founded the Rockefeller University in 1901; it was initially known as the Rockefeller Institute of Medical Research (1901–1958) and later known as the Rockefeller Institute (1958–1965). The University focuses on biological and medical sciences and provides education at the doctoral and post-doctoral levels. The University falls under the high research activity of higher education. The endowment fund of Rockefeller University was $2.2billion as of 2021. He also provided significant funding for Spelman College (formerly known as

Atlanta Baptist Female Seminary), renamed after Laura Spelman's (Rockefeller's wife's family name). Rockefeller also made significant donations to several Universities: Brown, Columbia, Harvard, and Yale.

Rockefeller was one of the founding members of the General Education Board—a non-governmental organization. It focused on supporting higher education in the rural black and white schools in the United States and modernizing farming practices in the Southern United States. One of his enduring legacies is the Rockefeller Foundation; it was founded in 1913. The foundation states its objectives as, *"Nourish people and the planet, ending energy poverty, expanding equity and economic opportunity, and seizing upon emerging frontiers."* The first grant made by the foundation was to the American Red Cross. Over the years, Rockefeller Foundation has supported public health research initiatives, vaccine development in yellow fever and malaria, and green revolution programs.

Rockefeller was also active in the financial support of church-based programs and institutions, especially the Baptist denomination, such as Denison University, formerly known as Granville college. He did not limit his philanthropic gesture to only the United States; the America Baptist Foreign Mission Society founded the Central Philippine University through grants made available by Rockefeller.

Baptist pastor Frederick Taylor Gates and John D. Rockefeller Jr.—his son—were his advisers on philanthropy matters. In most of the institutions he founded, both Gates and Rockefeller Jr. were listed as co-founders.

Rockefeller died on May 23, 1937, at a great age of 97 years, three years short of his target of 100 years. He gave out over $500million in various philanthropic programs in his lifetime. Rockefeller married Laura Celestia 'Cettie' Spelman; he lost her in 1915. They had five children, Elizabeth 'Bessie' Rockefeller, Alice Rockefeller, Alta Rockefeller, Edith Rockefeller, and John D. Rockefeller Jr. Only Alice, Alta, and John Jr. survived him.

Mother Teresa (1910–1997)

Mother Teresa was an exceptional woman; she left the comfort of her missionary establishment, the Loreto Sisters, and dedicated her life to helping the poor and the unloved in society. She founded the Order of the Missionaries of Charity on October 7, 1950, whose mission is *"to care for the hungry, the homeless, the crippled, the blind, the lepers, all the unwanted, unloved, uncatered for throughout society, people that have become a burden to the society and abandoned by everyone."*

Mother Teresa's foray into humanitarianism has its roots in her upbringing. She was born and baptized Agnes Gonxha Bojaxhiu in Skopje, the current capital of the Republic of Macedonia, to parents of Albanian descent. She lost her entrepreneurial and politically active father under unclear circumstances when she was eight years old. Her mother's strong belief in giving and sharing with the poor, no matter how little, largely influenced her. Mother Teresa always remembers her mother's counsel, *"My child, never eat a single mouthful unless you are sharing it with others."*

Young Agnes realized her religious calling at 12 years while on one of her pilgrimages to the shrine of the Black Madonna of Vitina-Letnice. In 1928, at 18 years, she set off to Rathfarnham, Dublin, Ireland, to join the Loreto Sisters, where she studied English. Teresa is a variant of Thérèse, named after Saint Thérèse of Lisieux. A year later, she went to India to join Loreto Sisters for her novitiate. After two years, she made her first religious vow and was assigned to Loreto Sisters' managed St. Mary High School for girls, where she taught history and geography.

On September 10, 1946, Mother Teresa encountered what she described as a *"Calling within a call,"* which changed her life completely. She claimed that she received instructions from Jesus Christ to leave teaching and work with the poorest and very sick people in the slums of Calcutta, India. It took her over a year of lobbying to get approval from the convent authorities to pursue her new calling.

After six months of basic medical training, Mother Teresa wandered into the slums of Calcutta, India, to help the poor, unwanted, and unloved.

The initial start was challenging for her; there were no structures and support systems. At some point, she was tempted to go back to the sheltered life of the Loreto Sisters, but somehow, she mustered inner strength and trudged on. Mother Teresa convinced government officials to use a dilapidated building to house the dying destitute, and she started an open-air school. She got personnel support from former teachers and pupils of St. Mary High School. Shortly after, her work gained attention, and help poured in from all corners. Mother Teresa established orphanages, a leper colony, nursing homes, and mobile clinics. Between 1971 and 1985, she founded a charity home in New York and another in Beirut, Lebanon. In her lifetime, she established over 500 charity homes in over 100 countries worldwide.

Mother Teresa had her share of controversies; she spoke out against contraception, divorce, and abortion. She received lots of flak for her position in such matters. She was also criticized for not doing enough in the homes the Order of Missionaries of Charity run. The detractors believe that despite all the funding she gets, supplies for food and medicines were below expectation; residents in pain were not given enough pain killers, making them suffer avoidable agonies.

Towards the end of her life, Mother Teresa battled several health challenges: pneumonia, heart problems, a domestic accident that broke her collarbone, and malaria. She died of a heart attack on September 5, 1997, leaving behind a functional mission with 4,000 sisters and 300 associate brothers.

Wealth or Humanity?

Mansa Musa ruled the Mali Empire in the 14th century; Andrew Carnegie and John D. Rockefeller strutted the American steel and oil industries like a colossus, and both between the 19th and 20th centuries. Mother Teresa took charity to another level in the 20th century, starting from India, and it spread across the world in an unprecedented manner. I will review what has become of their wealth and their philanthropy endeavors in the present time.

Wealth—Mansa Musa

There is not much evidence of Mansa Musa's wealth in present-day Mali. Present-day Mali is about the same size as the Mali Empire in Mansa Musa's era, about 1.25 million kilometers square, but different territorial coverage. Mansa Musa's Mali Empire included Southern Mauritania, Senegal, Gambia, Guinea Bissau, Guinea, Ivory Coast, Northern Burkina Faso, Northern Ghana, and western Niger. Since Mansa Musa was an emperor, where there was familial continuity in leadership, he likely left his wealth in the hands of his successor. A possible trace of his family tree is the Keitas, who still regard themselves as the noble class in Mali; however, there are no DNA records to support such a claim. Also, the evidence of wealth passed on to them is non-existent. Another angle is to assess the level of development of the Mali Empire at that time; its robustness to be able to retain such humongous wealth.

Mansa Musa invested heavily in edifices, schools, and mosques, especially in Niani, Timbuktu, and Gao. He also brought in scholars in art, mathematics, law, and astrology; however, there was no proof of him developing a sustainable economic system to keep the empire's wealth aside from making towns like Gao and Timbuktu major trade routes. There was no evidence of industrial development; the empire's products were mainly extractive and agricultural: salt, gold, and elephant ivory.

Another thinking is that since he continually built mosques every Friday and attracted the best architects, astrologers, mathematicians, and jurists, the human resources would have been expensive to maintain. It is not unlikely that a sizeable amount of the empire's wealth was used up maintaining such a large, highly educated personnel size.

Another perspective is to trace the wealth of Mansa Musa to the cities he developed during his reign: Niani, Timbuktu, and Gao. Timbuktu and Gao are still in present-day Mali; they were a beehive of culture, education, religion, and commerce activities. Niani, which is in present-day Guinea, was the official capital of the empire. The economic system was not as developed as it is now, so it is unlikely that the wealth of Mansa Musa was transferred abroad. Going by what happened to his predecessor, Mansa Abubakari, America had not been discovered in Mansa Musa's era. There was no account of his significant interaction with other empires aside from his contact with Egypt and Mecca during his famous Holy pilgrimage to Mecca in 1324. Mansa Musa's visit to Mamluk Sultan of Egypt, Al-Nasir Muhammad, was more of a courtesy call during the famous Holy pilgrimage than an attempt at strengthening economic ties. Mansa Musa's reported connection with Europe is primarily his famed riches, where he was depicted in the Catalan Atlas of 1375 by Abraham Cresques.

Niani was the capital of the Mali Empire. It is along the bank of the Sankarani river: one of the tributaries of the River Niger in present-day Guinea. Mansa Musa's procession to the Holy pilgrimage to Mecca started in Niani. Niani achieved its highest splendor during the reign of Mansa Musa as it was the political, commercial, and caravan center of the empire. Niani was the empire's capital for up to 300 years, but Songhai cavalrymen raided it in the 15th century: it never recovered its splendor. Niani has since recoiled into a small town; pieces of evidence of its splendor and political relevance are from archaeological excavations. The excavations were initially done in the 1920s; it was repeated in 1965 and 1968 by Guinean and Polish archaeologists.

Timbuktu became part of the Mali Empire in the late 13th century. It flourished under Mansa Musa, who made it one of the vital learning, trade, cultural, and religious centers. He commissioned the great Djinguereber mosque in 1327, and one of his royal residences was also in Timbuktu. The Sankore mosques that later became Sankore University and Timbuktu University at different times are some landmark physical developments in Timbuktu during Mansa Musa's era. At its peak, Timbuktu had over 25,000 scholars and was a significant trade route. The current population of Timbuktu is 55,000, barely double the number of scholars during its peak. The Djinguereber mosque is the only significant evidence of its glorious past.

Gao was recaptured from the Songhai Empire in 1325 by the Mali Empire while Mansa Musa was on his way back from the famous pilgrimage to Mecca. To emphasize the significance of Gao to the Mali Empire, Mansa Musa reportedly made a detour and visited Gao. He took the two sons of Gao's King, Ali Kolon and Suleiman Nar; Mansa Musa educated them outside of Gao. Mansa Musa developed Gao and continued to use it as one of the major trading routes in the Empire of Mali. The Songhai Empire later recaptured it after four decades. Irrespective of the kingdom that controlled the town, it continued to be a significant trade route for copper, gold, salt, and slaves in the region. Gao's relevance as a commercial hub waned after its capture by the Moroccans in the 16th century from the Songhai Empire. The only enduring evidence of its glorious past is the tomb of Songhai Emperor, Askia Mohammed, constructed in 1495 and designated as a UNESCO world heritage site.

Different reasons may have accounted for the loss of the wealth of the Mali Empire in subsequent years: unsustainable capital projects, Mansa

Musa built a mosque every Friday including other edifices, subsequent Mansas may have towed the same line; plunder from invaders—Touareg in 1433, Songhai in the 16th, and Moroccan army also in the 16th century—and the desertification of some of the agricultural lands, may have undermined the food security of the once flourishing empire.

Mansa Musa died in 1337, and his son, Mansa Maghan, took over the reins of power. Mansa Musa's wealth was likely passed on to Mansa Maghan, who may have passed it on to other Mansas that succeeded him. A review of the map of present-day Mali shows that Gao and Timbuktu are in the middle of present-day Mali. It is safe to infer that a good portion of present-day Mali was part of the Mansa Musa's Mali Empire. Reviewing the economy of present-day Mali as of 2021, it falls in the middle in terms of Gross Domestic Product (GDP) and the per capita income in Africa, but it is at the lower rung in the world. It implies that if Mansa Musa's wealth was left in present-day Mali, it might have been frittered away through mismanagement by subsequent Mansas, plundered by successive invaders, or lost as economic systems changed globally.

After tracing Mansa Musa's wealth through Niani, Timbuktu, Gao, and present-day Mali, it is apparent that there is little or no evidence of his wealth left. Only monuments like the Djinguerebor mosque in Timbuktu, which has only religious and cultural values, but insignificant economic value except for futuristic tourism potential.

Wealth—Andrew Carnegie

Andrew Carnegie's wealth is straightforward to trace; he is often referred to as the father of modern philanthropy. In 1901, after making his fortunes in the steel industry, he sold Andrew Carnegie steel to J.S. Morgan's promoted United Steel Corporation for $480million for a 5% 50-year-old bond; Carnegie's share of the proceeds was $230million.

Carnegie gave out over $350million of his wealth to different causes in his lifetime.

Wealth—John D. Rockefeller

At the peak of Rockefeller's career, he controlled over 90% of the oil industry in the world. He is arguably the wealthiest American that has ever lived, valued at $400billion in the current era. His growth created a monopolistic status for his company, Standard Oil, that pitted him against the United States authorities over antitrust law infringements. Rockefeller gave out over $500million of his fortune to charity during his lifetime.

Wealth—Mother Teresa

During my quest, I did not come across any record of Mother Teresa's wealth. It appears that all the money she generated was towards the Order of the Missionaries of Charity. Two cases of note support my position: First, in 1964, when Pope John Paul VI visited India and gave her the Lincoln Continental that American Catholics donated during the papal visit, she raffled it. Mother Teresa got more money than she would have realized if she had sold the vehicle in the open market, and she used the money to build a leprosy hospital in India. Second, in 1979, she won a Nobel prize for peace; the prize money was $190,000. She used the money to develop homes for her maturing children.

Humanity—Mansa Musa

Mansa Musa was a supremely generous man; this made him famous worldwide. In 1337, Al-Umari, a historian who visited Egypt, said Mansa Musa's praises had not subsided following his activities during his pilgrimage to Mecca in 1324. That stresses the impact of Mansa Musa's philanthropist gestures. One can only imagine how many families he lifted out of poverty by that singular procession. The pilgrimage to Mecca is the most conspicuous act of generosity of Mansa Musa that was documented; there could have been several other unreported acts. Nonetheless, that singular act that happened about seven centuries ago is still a topic of interest up till the present day.

Humanity—Andrew Carnegie

Andrew Carnegie did not only believe in philanthropy; he practiced and advocated it. He also developed his standard of philanthropy that still serves as a guiding principle; it appears that some billionaires in the current era use Carnegie's principles as a standard for their charity work. He wrote several essays and articles about giving, where he shared his thoughts and beliefs about philanthropy. In one of his popular essays turned book, *the gospel of wealth,* published in 1889, Andrew Carnegie made some recommendations:

- Modest living for the wealthy
- Recirculation of surplus wealth for the common good of humanity
- Selective giving with a focus on achieving maximum impact in society.

Carnegie gave out $350million, almost all his fortune, during his lifetime. He funded the construction of over 2,800 public libraries, donated over 8,000 organs to different churches, funded the Carnegie Institute of Science and Carnegie Mellon University, built an art theater, set up Carnegie Corporation, and founded the Carnegie Foundation. The Carnegie Foundation focused on advanced teaching and improvement in education, while he set up Carnegie Corporation to continue funding educational causes after his demise. He also developed architectural guidelines for developing public buildings that will foster efficiency. Most of the public institutions are still functional because he backed them with endowment funds to run autonomously.

Bill and Melinda Gates and Warren Buffett's founded *Giving Pledge* aligns with Andrew Carnegie's writings. The *Giving Pledge* is an open invitation for the world's wealthiest to commit to giving out at least 50% of their wealth, either in their lifetime or in their wills towards solving the world's most pressing problems. At the onset, 40 Americans committed to the pledge. As of 2021, over 200 individuals and families have pledged from 25 countries globally.

Humanity—John D. Rockefeller

John D. Rockefeller and Andrew Carnegie are of the same era. Carnegie's philanthropist effort may have influenced Rockefeller. He made significant donations to several institutions during his lifetime: Spelman College, Denison, Central Philippine, Brown, Columbia, Harvard, and Yale Universities. Rockefeller was a founding member of the General Education Board. He also founded the Rockefeller Foundation in 1913. Rockefeller gave out over $500million of his fortune. Most of the institutions he founded or was a founding member of are still functional as of 2021.

Humanity—Mother Teresa

Mother Teresa was a personification of humanity. Following her conviction, she abandoned her comfort zone (Loreto Sisters) and went into the streets of Calcutta, India, with no money or structures to care for the dying and unloved in the society. Mother Teresa founded the Order of the Missionaries of Charity. She started what she described as the *'Calling within a Call'* to care for the sick,

dying, hungry, needy, and unloved in society. At her demise, the Missionaries of Charity has over 500 charity homes in over 100 countries worldwide, supported by over 4,000 volunteer sisters and 300 associated brothers.

Wealth or Humanity, which has a longer-lasting legacy?

I have reviewed Mansa Musa's wealth and found no trace of it after seven centuries. Andrew Carnegie gave out most of his wealth during his lifetime. After his demise, Carnegie routed his undistributed wealth through Carnegie Corporation, another organization formed to pursue several of his causes of interest. John D. Rockefeller gave out a substantial part of his wealth during his lifetime but left behind significant stakes in the government-initiated companies. I see Rockefeller's approach as a win-win on both the humanity angle and the family end because he gave out substantial funds with impact and still left considerable wealth for his family. Mother Teresa's only family was the Missionaries of Charity; she appears to have disconnected from her nuclear family when she joined the Loreto Sisters at 18 years. If she had any assets when she died, they were likely passed on to the mission.

Mansa Musa's humanity was portrayed at its best during the Holy pilgrimage to Mecca in 1324; He gave out substantial quantities of gold bars at every stop en route to Cairo and Mecca. For the gold bars to be enough to cause the devaluation of gold for over a decade shows that a substantial amount of gold got into the hands of individuals who readily disposed of them. I surmise that the future prosperity of several families may have been enhanced by that uncommon show of benevolence by the emperor; however, there are no records to assess the depth of the impact.

Andrew Carnegie's humanity has outlived him through the causes he funded, especially his building of public libraries; one can imagine how many people benefitted from them. His essays and articles continue to impact the world; specific actions of the current billionaires appear to have been shaped by Andrew Carnegie's teaching through his writings. The *Giving Pledge*, arguably the most audacious giving program in contemporary time, can be linked to Andrew Carnegie's teachings.

John D. Rockefeller appears to have struck a balance between giving and leaving substantial wealth for his family. Both his philanthropy and his wealth have outlived him.

Mother Teresa's approach was impactful, but I am skeptical of its sustainability. I did not come across any record of endowments to cater to the over 500 charity homes spread worldwide. Since she died, I am not aware of any person or persons who have been able to bring the work of Missionaries of Charity to people's consciousness the way Mother Teresa did. It is still a bit early to judge how long the Missionaries of Charity can carry on its objectives in the absence of Mother Teresa.

In conclusion, humanity is a thing of the heart; it appears that it is more difficult to destroy than wealth. It also seems to be more replicable by the people who benefited from it. I reminded us earlier of how Andrew Carnegie built several libraries following the impact of Col. James Anderson's influence on his life. In several cases, the people who draw inspiration from philanthropy may not have benefitted directly from the gesture, but they can evaluate the long-term impact of such actions. Not all the 200 billionaires that are signatories to the *Giving Pledge* may have benefitted directly from Andrew Carnegie's public libraries, but they can see value in his strategy. Carnegie's actions and that of other philanthropists can be inspirations to others. Institutions such as foundations and Universities appear to have a long lifespan if they have endowment funds. Learning from John D. Rockefeller, wealth left with companies that have a good structure and sustainable future in terms of products and services tends to last long as well. Most of the government-enforced offshoot companies from Standard Oil are still operating to the present day.

11 WEALTH OR KNOWLEDGE, WHICH HAS A LONGER-LASTING LEGACY?

"Legacy is not leaving something for people. It is leaving something in people."

................*Peter Strople*

The general practice is that wealth acquired in one's lifetime is bequeathed to dependents. The rationale behind the thinking is that achieving a wealthy status should liberate the family from poverty in the foreseeable future. Wealth, when gained legally, bestows on the person who earned it certain status and reverence in the society. Close relatives usually enjoy similar adoration along with the wealthy. If the wealth remains in the family, they will continue to enjoy the reverence. It would continue if the wealth bequeathed does not diminish in value or continues to generate good cash flow. For instance, bequests of shares in companies diminish in value if they go bankrupt or get involved in a scandal, especially if they are publicly quoted. I will explore the wealth and knowledge of three personalities: Mansa Musa and Andrew Carnegie, whom I have reviewed their legacies in the previous chapter, and include Albert Einstein to give us insight into which, Wealth or Knowledge, that has a longer-lasting legacy?

Mansa Musa

I have explored the exploits of Mansa Musa in the previous chapter. Recall that Mansa Musa was immensely wealthy; he purportedly was the richest man that ever lived. I traced the wealth of Mansa Musa to Niani (the capital of the Mali Empire), Timbuktu, Gao (the commercial, religious, cultural, and educational centers), Keita's family, and present-day Mali. There is no significant evidence of Mansa Musa's wealth after seven centuries; the few indications of his wealth are the Djinguereber mosque and the University of Sankore. The economic value the two great monuments might have is the tourism potential they could attract if adequately harnessed.

At the height of Mansa Musa's reign, Mali Empire, especially Timbuktu, attracted several students, including 25,000 mathematicians, astrologers, and jurists. Most of these professionals were involved in the Sankore Madrasa (Arabic word used to describe academic institutions, whether circular or religious), which later became Sankore University. The University of Sankore was a uniquely run independent schools or colleges. An Imam heads each of these schools, and classes usually take place in the open or in mosques.

The University had a combined library of over 700,000 manuscripts. The number of books gave Timbuktu the moniker, the city of books. The manuscripts formed the fulcrum of the learning resources in the University. While the city of Timbuktu declined, people, including scholars, left the city; the books were, however, preserved in hidden mud walls. The single known most extensive collection is 18,000 in Ahmed

Baba Institute, while they scattered the others in the city's many libraries. In 2018, UNESCO started the Timbuktu manuscript project to catalog and preserve the manuscripts. The city of Timbuktu may have lost its splendor and appeal, but not its reputation as a custodian of knowledge. The University of Sankore is one of the first universities in the world, dating back to 989AD. The chief judge of Timbuktu set it up, and it became prominent during Mansa Musa's reign when he brought in scholars: mathematicians, astrologers, and jurists.

Andrew Carnegie

Andrew Carnegie developed the steel industry in the United States in the nineteenth and twentieth centuries; he became the biggest steel producer worldwide during this period. Aside from business, Carnegie was also a lover of books and a prolific writer; he continually contributed articles to the newspapers of his time. Carnegie authored several books: *The Gospel of Wealth, Advantages of Poverty, The Autobiography of Andrew Carnegie, Round the World, The Empire of Business, Triumphant Democracy, An American Four-In-Hand in Britain, The Advantages of Poverty, A League of Peace, and James Watt.* Carnegie's books are one part of his contributions to the advancement of knowledge; other notable contributions are the development of the steel industry and the advancement of knowledge through his philanthropy causes such as public libraries, universities, and research centers. I will review his effort in advancing knowledge by focusing on his article turned book, *The Gospel of Wealth*. I summarized below his views on how the wealthy can relate with the public for the greater good of humankind as enunciated in the book:

o There are three ways that surplus wealth can be disposed of:
  i) To the families of the descendants
  ii) Bequeathed for a public purpose
  iii) Administered during the lifetime of the possessor
o The wealthy's surplus should not be applied to their families or descendants but bequeathed for a public purpose

o Bequeathing money to the family of the deceased is the most injustice

o Carnegie asked a pertinent question, why do men leave a substantial fortune to their children, is it misguided affection?

o Great wealth bequeathed often works for the injury of the legatee than for their good

o Men who cannot educate their children to earn a living will leave them in poverty

o Most bequests are more of the retention of family pride than the welfare of the children

o Bequeathing wealth for public use may not achieve the purpose as the bequeather will not properly supervise it

o It takes an equal amount of energy used in acquiring wealth to achieve a set objective with the wealth

o He supports an increased tax on the estate of the dead and believes that increased tax on the dead will motivate the dead to give away their wealth in their lifetime

o He disagrees with sharing the wealth in small bits to the general populace

o The wealthy should live in modesty and shun extravagance

o The wealthy should provide moderately for their dependents

o The wealthy should administer surplus wealth for the common good of humankind

o The man of wealth is a mere agent and trustee of the less endowed public

o He described modest funds accumulated over time through moderate savings as a product of competence, and it differs from wealth

o He advised that every society should aspire to achieve a modicum of competence

o Bequests left by the dead for public use leaves the money idle through delays in administering the will and legal contentions of the will

o For every $1,000 spent on charities, $950 is wasted and produces the evil it was designed to mitigate o We should discourage indiscriminate giving; instead, giving should be purposeful

o Money given to beggars makes them idle; begging is a dishonorable way of living

o Giving money to establish great institutions in one's lifetime is preferable to bequeathing it, for it is merely living behind what one cannot carry to the grave

o It is the duty of the wealthy to administer the surplus within their lifetime rather than leaving the burden to somebody else

o Wealth should be used in six areas:
  i)   Founding and funding universities
  ii)   Free libraries
  iii) Founding or extension of hospitals
  iv)   Hall and theaters
  v)   Swimming pools
  vi)   Churches

o Everyone should contribute their quota to the public good no matter how small, at the very least, time and energy.

Carnegie would have ruffled several feathers with the above positions in the 19th century; in the 21st century, the majority of the excess wealth of the rich is still bequeathed to families.

Carnegie was not only an advocate of the principles; he practiced them. He gave out over 90% of his wealth, $350million during his lifetime. John D. Rockefeller appears to have bought into Carnegie's ideologies as he had just $21million in his estate at his death; he gave out over $500million of his fortune for different causes.

The *Giving Pledge* earlier mentioned aligns with Carnegie's position; the only difference is that signatories to the *Giving Pledge* have the liberty to either give out the assets now or bequeath them. Bequeathing assets is one area Carnegies opposed. He sees it as a delayed giving occasioned by the realization process; the will may be contested or delayed because of regular court proceedings. Carnegie believes that such delays would be avoided if the assets are given out in the bequeather's lifetime. The gospel of wealth was written over a century ago, but the world still benefits from the insightful knowledge embedded in the monumental work. As of 2021, the total wealth of all billionaires worldwide, according to Forbes, is $13.1 trillion. Imagine that 50% of that amount, $6.5 trillion, is pledged and judiciously used for the common good of humanity: education, climate change, research, and medicine. Somebody shared his thoughts on surplus wealth management; over a century later, the world is not only agreeing to the knowledge but acting on and benefitting from it. It brings us to another subject of storage, sharing, and retrieval of knowledge. Suppose Carnegie did not share his ideas? The milestone so far achieved by the *Giving Pledge* may not have occurred, including several other institutions and noble causes. Knowledge should be preserved as an endowment for the future generation; one may not know when the knowledge will be accessed and used for the common good of humankind.

Albert Einstein (1879–1955)

German-born Albert Einstein is of Jewish descent. He is a renowned mathematician and physicist with checkered academic training. Einstein had his elementary education in Germany; he later moved to Switzerland in 1896 to study physics and mathematics at the prestigious Swiss Federal Polytechnic. Einstein got his diploma in 1901 and gained Swiss citizenship the same year after forsaking his German citizenship. After graduation, he could not get a teaching position because one of his professors in the polytechnic, Heinrich Weber, gave him a below-par recommendation. Einstein was fond of missing classes; he preferred self-study to structured learning. Einstein had to pick up a clerical position in the Swiss Patent Office in 1902. The clerical job became a blessing in disguise; it gave Einstein ample time to study, research, and write. It was the golden period of his career; in 1905, he published four papers in the *Annalen der Physik*: one of that era's most popular physics journals.

Einstein was awarded a Ph.D. in 1905 by the University of Zurich. Between 1905 and 1921, he lectured at the University of Zurich, Prussia Academy of Sciences, Humboldt University of Berlin, and Karl-Ferdinand University in Prague. He also took non-teaching positions in the Eidgenössische Technische Hochschule in Zürich and Kaiser Wilhelm Institute of Physics in Berlin.

One of his profound theories is the matter/energy relationship, where he proposed the equation: $E=mc^2$, explained as the energy of a body (E) is equal to the mass (m) multiplied by the speed of light squared (c^2). The equation suggests that matter can be converted into energy much greater than the matter of its origin. The matter/energy relationship equation was the forerunner to atomic power and later the nuclear bomb.

In 1915, Einstein published the completed work on the theory of relativity that he started in 1905; the theory states that gravitational fields cause distortions in the fabric of space and time. It remained controversial until it was proven correct by the solar eclipse of 1919.

Einstein's simple explanation of the previously unexplained puzzle of the photoelectric effect earned him the Nobel prize for physics in 1921.

He alerted the United States government of Germany's effort towards building an atomic bomb and urged them to start their program, the Manhattan Project; nevertheless, Einstein was not directly involved. The Manhattan Project produced the two atomic bombs that the United States used in the two Japanese cities—Hiroshima and Nagasaki—during World War II; the bombs decimated both cities. Einstein later regretted his contribution in making the bombs and became an advocate of nuclear disarmament, urging dialogue in the place of war.

Einstein had deep connections with his Jewish roots. He often spoke up against anti-Semitism, but he was not a staunch Zionist. In 1952, following the death of the Israeli president, Chaim Weizmann, Israel offered him the presidency; Einstein declined, claiming a lack of aptitude and experience to deal with people at that level and in performing official functions. Through Einstein's effort, over 1,000 Jewish scientists escaped from Germany and got positions in Turkish Universities during the early days of the pogrom of the Jews by the Germans.

Albert Einstein died in 1955, and his body was cremated at his behest, but Princeton Pathologist Thomas Harvey removed his brain during the autopsy under controversial circumstances. Harvey cut it into several pieces and sent them to different scientists for research. Upon examination, Canadian scientists found out that Einstein's inferior parietal lobule, the area that processes languages and mathematics, is 15% larger than usual; that might explain his exceptional intelligence.

Albert Einstein was not a man of much means, but his contribution to the world of physics set the tone for several discoveries that are still relevant to the present day.

Wealth or Knowledge, which has a longer-lasting legacy?

It is challenging to determine which, Wealth or Knowledge, has a longer-lasting legacy? However, it is tempting to say that knowledge has a longer-lasting legacy than wealth. Nonetheless, if wealth is channeled properly into knowledge acquisition, as with Mansa Musa, who used part of his wealth to develop Sankore University, he also funded the writing of several manuscripts that have survived the test of time. But if the wealth is used to acquire diminishing assets such as buildings, cars, and other luxuries of life, they will not last as long as knowledge. Knowledge can be replicated, expanded, and transferred more easily than wealth. In addition, the wealth that is distributed diminishes if the people sharing it increase, unless the beneficiaries can replicate the wealth.

Knowledge appears to increase when shared amongst several people; they will likely improve on it. In 1921, Albert Einstein won a Nobel Prize for physics for explaining the photoelectric effect. It is noteworthy that

Einstein did not discover the photoelectric effect; Heinrich Rudolf Hertz, a German physicist, discovered it in 1887 but left an unexplained puzzle that Albert Einstein's equation explained.

12 HOW TO REPAIR NEGATIVE LEGACY

*'It's not how we make mistakes, but how we
correct them that defines us.''*
.... *Rachel Wolchin*

Negative legacy comes with burdens; this could be regret following self-appraisal, backlash from society, continuous bashing by the press, or prosecution from the authorities. The burden of negative legacies could lead to depression, and at the extreme, suicide. The repercussions of the legacy do not end with the root legacy; it could extend to the family, country, and continent. It is a liability that can mutate and affect several groups of people simultaneously. Before I delve into the topic of repairing negative legacies, I will explore some examples of negative legacies.

Persons with negative legacies

Over the years, several people have acquired negative legacies, enough to fill up more than a book title. I singled out personalities from different continents of the world. My pick may not be a hideous negative legacy in your view, as legacies are essentially a function of individual perception. For instance, until the death of Pablo Escobar's mother, Hermilda Gaviria de Escobar, she continually insisted that her son, Pablo, one of the most notorious drug barons in the twentieth century, was not a criminal. She saw him as Pablo, her son, while the world saw him as Pablo, the drug baron. She was unabashed about her position. Hermilda regularly and openly visited Pablo's tomb until she died in 2006. The preceding narrative explains the perception effect of legacies.

Adolf Hitler (1889–1945)

Adolf Hitler was a German leader of Austrian descent; he was the protagonist of World War II, which lasted for six years (1939–1945). Hitler is from a modest background; he developed early German nationalist ideologies that made him join politics, NSDAP (National Socialist German Workers Party, colloquially known as the Nazi party). A combination of anti-Semitism, German nationalism, and strong-willed nature turned him into the dictator he later became. Traces of Adolf's strong-mindedness can be found in his constant disagreement with his father, Alois Hitler, who made failed attempts to change Adolf's career path; Alois wanted Adolf to join the customs service and a technical school at different times. Adolf deliberately performed poorly in the technical school to protest his father's decision against him attending a classical high school where he wanted to pursue his artistic desires. Supported by hindsight, if Alois had allowed Adolf to pursue his creative dreams, the world might have been saved from the carnage of World War II.

Adolf Hitler voluntarily joined the Bavarian army to prosecute World War I in 1914. World War I lasted about four years (1914–1918). In the conflict, Germany, Austria-Hungary, Bulgaria, and the Ottoman Empire joined forces against the allied powers (Great Britain, France, Russia, Italy, Japan, Romania, and later, the United States).

Allowing Hitler to serve in the Bavarian (A territory in Germany that termed itself the Free States with common roots) army was an error by the authorities. Hitler was an Austrian citizen; he was not qualified to join the Bavarian army. World War I ended with an armistice offered by Germany on November 11, 1918; it was technically termed a defeat to the German army because of the lopsidedly crafted Treaty of Versailles: they curtailed German military expansion and took away some of its territories. The Treaty did not go down well with a host of German troops and citizens; they viewed the truce as accepting defeat by the civilian rulers but not necessarily a military defeat. The perceived failure by the ruling class formed some of Hitler's ideologies, and he used the general perception as a political tool to gain power and acceptance.

Hitler remained in the Bavarian army till March 31, 1920; he resigned and went into full-time politics. Along with General Erich Ludendorff and other accomplices, Hitler had a brief stint in prison after a conviction for high treason following his involvement in a failed coup attempt on November 9, 1923. On December 20, 1924, the German government released Hitler on parole; he became active in politics again. Through various political maneuvers within the Nazi party, Hitler became Chancellor on January 30, 1933, and the Chancellor and the head of government on August 2, 1934.

Hitler oversaw the German arms build-up; Germany signed a tripartite pact with Japan and Italy. Later, the pact was expanded to include Hungary, Romania, and Bulgaria; the countries were dubbed *Axis Powers*.

Germany started World War II by first attacking Poland in conjunction with the Soviet Union on September 1, 1939. It was followed by an attack on Denmark, Norway, Luxembourg, and France. Following Britain's rejection of Germany's peace overtures, Germany attacked Britain.

The belief is that Hitler shot himself on April 30, 1945, ostensibly to avoid the humiliation of being arrested by the advancing Soviet Army. Hitler initiated a war that caused the death of 86 million people, including 6 million Jews. Hitler has one of the most obnoxious legacies in global history.

Pablo Escobar (1949–1993)

Pablo Escobar grew up and operated his drug cartel in Medellin, Colombia's second-largest city. Pablo was a college dropout; he went through the ranks of crime: stealing and reselling gravestones, selling fake college degrees, contraband cigarettes, and fake lottery tickets. Pablo later graduated into car theft and kidnapping for ransom before delving into illicit drugs and forming the Medellin cartel.

He was notorious for bribing or killing police officers, judges, government officials, and politicians that stood in his way. He left his opponents with two tough choices, *"take silver or take lead,"* meaning you either take a bribe or get shot.

The cocaine was processed in Colombia and moved to the United States through the Bahamas. They started using the Panama route when Norman's Cay, the Bahamian Islands that used to be their transit point to the United States, had to be given up by its owner—Carlos Lehder—resulting from pressure from the United States' authorities. The illicit drug trade later took an international dimension; they had supply routes in Mexico, Europe, Asia, and Africa. At the peak of their activities, the Medellin cartel shipped out about 15 tons of cocaine per day; the cartel made up to $55million daily, amounting to over $20billion annually. The government seized a sizeable amount, some were lost in hiding, and rodents destroyed the rest.

Pablo built a 7,000-acre fortress, Hacienda Napoles, which later became his operational headquarters; he equipped it with several luxuries: swimming pools, airstrip, football pitch, bullfighting ring, an artificial lake, and zoo. The zoo boasted many exotic animals: elephants, giraffes, hippopotamus, camels, zebras, and ostriches.

Pablo was a man of complex disposition; he was ruthless in his dealings with rival gangs, persons, or institutions that stood in his way. However, he was a caring father and husband, but at the same time, a womanizer.

Pablo had no emotional attachment to any of his mistresses aside from his wife. Pablo once ordered the killing of one of his ex-mistresses, Wendy Chavarriaga Gil, when he discovered that she was an informant. Pablo was also a philanthropist; he built several schools, hospitals, houses for the poor, and sponsored soccer teams. His philanthropy endeared him to the people. Pablo won an election to an alternate seat in Colombia's congress in 1982; nevertheless, he had to resign because of his criminal past for fear of being publicly exposed.

In June 1991, Pablo turned himself in for a five-year negotiated imprisonment under favorable terms: non-extradition to the United States for trial, building his prison, and choosing his bodyguards. His purpose-built prison, *La Catedral*, was more of a resort than a prison; Pablo equipped it with a waterfall, sauna, nightclub, soccer field, and several other amenities. He continued his criminal activities in the facility. As his activities leaked to the press, it became an embarrassment to the Colombian government. Matters came to a head when he tortured and killed two cartel members within the facility. In July 1992, The Colombian government decided to move him to a less luxurious facility and cut down on his excesses. Pablo got wind of the government plan; he escaped from *La Catedral* and became a fugitive.

Unknown to him, he played into the hands of Colombian and United States governments whose hands he had tied with the initial arrangement. While on the run, he tried to negotiate another deal through his lawyers, but the government was not ready to deal with him again. Pablo tried moving his family out of Colombia severally, but the authorities turned them back; the authorities needed them as bait to get him.

On December 2, 1993, while Pablo was on a call to his son through a radiotelephone, the Search Bloc headed by one of his main adversaries in government, Brigadier Hugo Martinez, tracked his location using trilateration technology. After suffering a controversial fatal gunshot wound to the ear, Pablo died following a firefight with the Colombian National Police. That closed the chapter of Pablo Escobar's Medellin

Cartel. The cartel became fragmented, and the Cali cartel took over the Medellin cartel's territories.

Pablo's reign of terror claimed the lives of up to 4,000 people, including about 1,000 police officers, 200 judges, several journalists, an attorney general, and three presidential candidates.

Pablo Escobar left behind a legacy of narco-terrorism with blood and tears flowing in the streets of Medellin. Fast forward to now, the blood and tears left behind by Pablo Escobar may have dried up, but the memories still linger.

Idi Amin (1925–2003)

Idi Amin is arguably one of the most brutal despots that have come out of Africa; he ruled Uganda from 1971 to 1979. Idi Amin was an uneducated Ugandan of minority Kakwa ethnic extraction; he joined the Ugandan army as a cook during the British rule in 1946. Idi Amin was one of the first two Ugandans to be commissioned as officers in the Ugandan army in 1961. Following the independence of Uganda in 1962 from Britain, Idi Amin rose rapidly to become the commander of the armed forces in 1970. Although unlettered, Idi Amin was a successful athlete; he participated in swimming, rugby, and boxing. Idi Amin held the Ugandan light heavyweight championship belt for nine years (1951–1960).

Idi Amin's foray into politics has its roots in his association with Milton Obote, Uganda's first prime minister. Obote had a gold, ivory, and arms smuggling racket with Idi Amin that was exposed. Obote, through Idi Amin, attacked and forced the ceremonial president, Kabaka (King) Edward Mutesa II of Buganda, into exile in Britain. The action cemented Obote's position as the president with executive powers to avoid investigation from the parliament. Obote promoted Idi Amin to colonel and the head of the armed forces. Following damning evidence of Idi Amin's corrupt and disloyal activities, Obote reduced his portfolio to only the head of the army.

Two events led to a putsch by Idi Amin: a report of embezzlement that got to the ears of President Milton Obote and Obote's attempted assassination. Obote began to question Idi Amin's loyalty; Amin's arrest became imminent. In January 1971, Obote went to Singapore for the Commonwealth Summit; in his absence, Idi Amin seized power through a coup d'état.

Idi Amin courted the support of the Uganda populace through some reconciliatory and endearing actions in the early days of his leadership: he freed political prisoners; held a state funeral for Kabaka (King) Edward Mutesa II of Buganda, who had died in exile in Britain following Milton Obote's disposition; declared that he was a soldier, not a politician; and promised to return Uganda to civilian rule within five years.

Idi Amin's putsch initially had the blessings of the British government because Milton Obote's government was tilting towards communism. However, Idi Amin's initial posture soon proved to be a mere landing pad as subsequent events and actions exposed his original ambitions. He declared himself the president and commander-in-chief of the armed forces, suspended part of the constitution, and subjected the inducted civilian cabinet ministers to military control and discipline. Idi Amin issued about 30 decrees during his regime. He set up the State Research Bureau (SRB), the military police, and Public Safety Unit (PSU). The SRB replaced the intelligence agency of the former government, the General Service Unit (GSU). The SRB became an agency of torture and execution of anyone Idi Amin perceived as an enemy: whether real or imagined.

Idi Amin's brutal regime can be assessed from two angles: persecution of ethnic and political groups and economic wars. The persecution of ethnic and political groups is interrelated; the deposed political leader, Milton Obote, is of Lango ethnic descent. The military personnel of Lango and Ocholi extraction still supported Obote. Idi Amin destroyed that support base by ordering the massacre of over 5,000 Lango and Ocholi soldiers in Jinja and Mbarara barracks in 1971. The persecution did not end with the Lango and Ocholi soldiers; the spate of killings extended to other ethnic groups cutting across judges, intellectuals, bureaucrats, politicians, lawyers, students, journalists, criminal suspects, and government officials. At the end of his regime, he killed between 300,000 to 500,000 Ugandans and foreigners; often, Amin's agents dumped their remains in River Nile.

Notable victims of Idi Amin's regime are Benedicto Kiwanuka, a former minister; Joseph Mubiru, the former governor of the central bank; Frank Kalimuzo, the vice-chancellor of Makerere University; Erinayo Oryema and Oboth Ofumbi, two of his cabinet ministers; Janani Luwum, the Anglican archbishop; and a host of other prominent citizens.

During Idi Amin's regime, the spate of killings led several Ugandans to seek refuge in neighboring countries. Tanzania welcomed over 20,000 Ugandan refugees, where they joined the exiled former president, Milton Obote, and plotted coup attempts to regain power. All the coup attempts failed primarily because of poor execution; Idi Amin also replaced most top-ranking officers in the military and the cabinet with his cronies.

The economic war policy of Idi Amin's regime dates to Milton Obote's regime; Idi Amin was an integral part of that regime. It appears to be a product of a nationalistic consciousness infused with ingrained *Indophobia* that was developed over the years. During Obote's administration, he started nationalizing several privately-owned companies; these companies were mainly owned by the British. Idi Amin's economic war was a continuation of Obote's nationalization policy but with a focus on the Asian population. The Asians, mainly Indians, had been doing business in Uganda since the British colonial era.

The coming of the Indians to Uganda dates back to late 1800, during the construction of the Ugandan railway. The British brought over 30,000 Indians into Uganda to work as laborers in Uganda's railway project. After completing the projects, about 20% of the laborers stayed in Uganda to engage in other economic activities. Aside from the Indian railway laborers, as a deliberate policy, the British brought in several Indians to the then Ugandan protectorate to be involved in commerce and administration in preference to the Ugandans. As of 1971, when Idi Amin seized power, the South Asian population, which was predominantly Indians, was about 80,000, representing slightly less than 1% of Uganda's population. However, they controlled over 20% of the Ugandan economy. The lopsided distribution of Uganda's wealth birthed the *Indophobia* malady. In 1972, Idi Amin issued a decree expelling Asians who were not Uganda citizens from Uganda; about 60,000 Asians fell into this category. The mass exodus saw roughly 50% of them moving to the United Kingdom; the rest moved to Australia, Kenya, Canada, South Africa, Fiji, India, Pakistan, Tanzania, Sweden, and the United States. After the mass exodus, the Ugandan government started expropriating the assets left behind by the Asians; Idi Amin shared the assets between the state and his cronies. Ugandans were ill-equipped to manage the sudden fortune.

Soon, industries began to collapse because of poor management; Uganda also acquired a pariah status in the international community. As a result, the Ugandan economy faltered, and inflation set in. A scene that appears to be a parody in one of the related movies, *"The rise and fall of Idi Amin,"* portrayed Idi Amin's ignorance of the workings of the economy when he asked the governor of the central bank of Uganda for money. The governor responded that the government was broke; Idi Amin then instructed the governor to print more paper notes. The governor explained that if he printed more paper notes, Uganda's money would be like tissue paper (meaning that it would lose its value). Idi Amin retorted, *"You call Ugandan money tissue paper? Take him away."* Take him away in that movie meant go and kill him. I do not have any evidence of this incident occurring during Idi Amin's regime, but the parody was insightful. It exposed Idi Amin's ignorance of the workings of the economy, the severity of the collapse of Uganda's economy, and his cruelty; he could kill anyone with the slightest provocation without recourse to the rule of law.

Although Idi Amin's regime started on a sound footing, his rule soon became an embarrassment to Ugandans and Africa in general. Idi Amin severed relations with Britain, Israel, India, Tanzania, Kenya but courted the Soviet Union, East Germany, and Libya.

Idi Amin's involvement in the infamous hijack of an Air France airliner from Tel Aviv, Israel, to Paris is palpable. The Popular Front for the Liberation of Palestine (PFLP) members ordered the hijack. Idi Amin allowed the hijacked airplane to land in Entebbe airport in Uganda, and his body language appeared to have supported the hijackers. The general belief is that Idi Amin was aware of the hijack from the outset; he visited the hostages almost daily to brief them on the progress made with the negotiations: a deceptive show of statesmanship. Idi Amin provided security cover at the airport for the hijackers. Despite an appeal by Israel to Idi Amin through contacts within Israel for help with the hostage situation, Idi Amin did not bulge.

On July 3, 1976, Israel took matters into its hands by sending commandos in an operation codenamed *Operation Thunderbolt* but popularly referred to as *Operation Entebbe*. The operation lasted barely an hour, and the Israeli commandos freed 102 out of the 106 hostages. Three of the hostages died, and they left behind one hostage, 74-year-old Dora Bloch; she had been taken to the hospital after choking on a chicken bone. Idi Amin's forces allegedly killed her in retaliation for Israel's action.

The Ugandan soldiers' estimated casualty was four dozen; 11 Soviet-built MiG-17 and MiG-21 fighter planes of the Uganda Air Force were destroyed. The Israeli commandos allegedly destroyed the Ugandan fighter jets not to be scrambled to chase the Israeli rescue aircraft. The casualties on the Israeli side included the assault unit commander, Yonatan Netanyahu (the elder brother of Israel's former prime minister Benjamin Netanyahu) was killed, and five commandos including ten hostages were wounded.

A series of events led to the deposition of Idi Amin in 1979. First, two factions evolved in the army, a section loyal to the vice president, General Mustapha Adrisi, and the other to Idi Amin. Second, Amin's support base shrank because of the harsh economic realities, hostile political environment, and general insecurity. In early 1978, General Adrisi was involved in a near-fatal car accident that the supporters believed was a failed assassination attempt; he was flown to Cairo, Egypt, for medical treatment. While in Egypt, the government stripped him of two of his portfolios: defense and home affairs. Later the same year, troops loyal to General Adrisi mutinied, and a fight broke out between Amin's troops and Adrisi's loyalists along the Ugandan-Tanzanian border. The Ugandan army subsequently invaded Tanzanian territory (Idi Amin's purported strategy to shift attention from the internal economic and political crisis). Under the leadership of Julius Nyerere, the Tanzanian government mobilized and supported several Ugandan exiles through the Uganda National Liberation Army (UNLA). Despite support from Libya, Amin's forces retreated continuously until April 11, 1979, when Idi Amin fled to exile in Libya. The Tanzanian-led forces captured Kampala, Uganda's capital. Idi Amin moved to Saudi Arabia in 1980 and was allowed to settle tas a guest of the royal family, provided he stayed out of politics.

Idi Amin conferred several titles on himself: Field Marshal, CBE (Conqueror of the British Empire), Lord of All the Beasts of the Earth and Fishes of the Seas, Uncrowned King of Scotland, Doctor of Law from Makerere University, and VC (Victorious Cross) amongst others.

Idi Amin was a polygamist; he married at least six wives and sired about 55 children. On July 19, 2003, Amin died from kidney failure at King Faisal Specialist Hospital and Research Center in Jeddah, Saudi Arabia. They buried him in a simple grave in Ruwais Cemetery in Jeddah with no honors usually accorded past heads of state.

The death of Idi Amin closed the chapter of one of the despotic, erratic, cruel, enigmatic, and militarized governments in modern history.

Abu Bakr al-Baghdadi (1971–2019)

Abu Bakr al-Baghdadi was an inconspicuous figure until he became the controversial caliph of the Islamic State (IS). He was born in Samarra in Iraq around 1971, the third child of four sons. Baghdadi acquired a doctorate in Islamic Studies from the Islamic University of Iraq, now known as Iraq University. People who had a good recollection of his persona described him as a hermit, shy, with a strong distaste for violence.

Although an Islamic scholar, Baghdadi's foray into Islamic radicalism is traceable to his joining Salafi-jihadi groups in Iraq after the US invasion of Iraq in 2003; he was detained for about a year along with al-Qaeda commanders in the United States' controlled Camp Bucca in Iraq. Baghdadi purportedly joined al-Qaeda during his detention in Camp Bucca. After Baghdadi's release, he became active in al-Qaeda and rose through the ranks until they appointed him an emir in 2010—the highest-ranking officer.

Baghdadi transmuted al-Qaeda in Iraq into the Islamic State in Iraq (ISI) and carried out several terrorist attacks in Iraq, mainly through suicide bombing. He did not spare mosques during his campaign of terror, necessitating the United States to place a $10million reward for information leading to his arrest in 2010 (they increased it to $25million in 2017).

ISI expanded into Syria to become ISIS (Islamic State of Iraq and Syria) against the directives of al-Qaeda leadership. In 2014, ISIS permanently broke away from al-Qaeda and renamed itself Islamic State (IS), declared itself a caliphate, and the Shura Council chose Baghdadi as the caliph. The Muslim and international community rejected the Islamic State's position; the United Nations and several other countries labeled the Islamic State a terrorist organization.

The international condemnation of the Islamic State's self-declaration did not deter Baghdadi from his expansionist ambitions; the Islamic State expanded into Iraq and Syria and conquered substantial territories. The Baghdadi-led Islamic State deployed extreme tactics to prosecute its wars; they used crude execution methods: beheading, drowning, burning, and stoning. Baghdadi oversaw all manners of atrocities and human rights violations, especially the genocide of the Yazidis, a minority group in Iraq. They killed several Yazidi men and turned their women into sex slaves. The Islamic State ruled the territories under their control with uttermost primitivity. They deprived residents of its domain of fundamental human rights; inhabitants lived continually in fear. Floggings, organized rape, forced marriages, sexual slavery, and public killings occurred daily. I can recollect the case of a young man they executed because they caught him listening to western music. When I read the story, I wondered what kind of offense is in listening to music. Assuming it is an offense by their judgment, should it carry the maximum penalty?

The Islamic State deployed propaganda to instill fear into its subjects and the territories they were about to attack. They made videos of different gory details of killings, sexual slavery, and all

manners of dehumanizing activities to drive home their capabilities.

Following the United States-led international military coalition in 2014, a direct response to the atrocities of the Islamic State against the Yazidis. By the end of 2017, the Islamic State had lost over 95% of the territories it once controlled, including its de facto capital Raqqa, Syria. Consequently, Baghdadi descended into a fugitive lifestyle.

On October 27, 2019, Baghdadi detonated a suicide vest, killing himself and two of his children during an air raid in Barisha, Idlib Province, Syria, by the United States forces; they buried him at sea. Later, the Islamic State confirmed his death and appointed Abu Ibrahim al-Hashimi al-Qurashi to head the organization.

Strategies to repair negative legacies

I have explored the negative legacies of four personalities: Adolf Hitler, Pablo Escobar, Idi Amin, and Abu Bakr al-Baghdadi spanning Europe, South America, Africa, and the Middle East. Three of the four cases died while pursuing their infamous ambitions; only Idi Amin died of natural causes—albeit, in exile and like a commoner. The preceding instances call for self-appraisal and sober reflection. Sadly, negative legacy does not end with the root legacy as we saw in chapter 2, Legacy types and levels. In the chapter, I pointed out that legacies transcend the root legacy and mutate to form family up to continental legacies. Even when the root legacy dies, the legacy continues to resonate; it either benefits other legacy levels or becomes a burden to them.

It is essential that we explore how negative legacies can be repaired. I have identified five strategies that people, or organizations have used to achieve it:

- Public admittance and apology
- Advocacy
- Reparations
- Dissociation
- Subsumption

Why repair negative legacies?

Before I discuss the negative legacy repair strategies, I will list below supporting arguments for repairing negative legacies.

i. For the root legacy, repairing negative legacies gives the source of the legacy the opportunity to right the wrongs; he may have inadvertently created or have realized the need to tow a positive legacy pathway by correcting the negative legacies he had earlier created. It gives the root legacy an opportunity for positive future action and a possible positive impact on society.

ii. As we saw in chapter 3, some legacies are accidental. The legacy might be negative, but it was probably not a deliberate attempt by the root legacy to create such a legacy. It could be a result of uncontrollable circumstances. It is fair that the root legacy is given the opportunity to right the wrongs.

iii. As mentioned earlier in chapter 4 and further expatiated later in this chapter, some legacies happen subconsciously. Granted that one may have been involved in the making of the legacy, but you were not conscious of the negative legacy implications. So, one could inadvertently create a negative legacy.

iv. It is also equitable for those associated with the root legacy, through other legacy levels, to give them a chance to repair the legacy. Successfully repairing such a negative legacy could help lessen the burden the legacy imposed on them.

v. Repair of negative legacy could alleviate the emotional suffering of the victims as well as reposition them economically.

1.   Public/private admittance and apology strategy

This strategy has been adopted several times; I will list a few of them below and examine their effects.

I. On December 7, 1970, Willy Brandt, then a foreign minister of West Germany, laid a wreath at the memorial of the Jewish ghetto in Poland in recognition of the pogrom of the Jews by the Germans. He fell to his knees and kept silent for almost half a minute; it was a public show of remorse. It is notable that Willy Brandt resisted Hitler and played no role in the pogrom, but his effort was an attempt to repair a negative legacy that has become a German burden.

II. On September 1, 2019, German president, Frank-Walter Steinmeier, expressed deep regret for the pain Germany inflicted on Poland during World War II and used two strong words to describe the German atrocities, *"German crime* and *Painful legacy."*

III. On December 2, 2013, Pablo Escobar's 20th death anniversary, the younger sister of Pablo, Luz Maria Escobar, held a mass at a Catholic church, Jardines Montesacro cemetery, in Medellin,

Colombia, where she publicly apologized for the sins of her brother. She also dropped notes on the tombs of Pablo's victims to ask for forgiveness. She has nothing to repent of personally; they did not involve her in the cartel, but she cannot shy away from her family's negative legacy orchestrated by Pablo. She is conscious of the pain and agony Pablo's actions have caused several families, and she wants to right the wrongs in any way she can.

In reviewing the effectiveness of the above strategy, countries like Poland appear to have accepted and moved on in the German case. However, pockets of remonstrations intermittently come up, especially in public events. It is not the case with Israeli citizens; the pain of the Germans' atrocities meted out to their forebearers is yet to abate. Several Israelis do not want to do anything with Germany; nonetheless, Israel and Western Germany established diplomatic relations in 1965. Germany and Israel are currently significant trade partners and have strong military ties.

In Luz Maria Escobar's effort, some Colombians applaud her attempt as a soothing balm to the pain inflicted on innocent Colombian citizens by her brother, Pablo. However, only a few of the victim's relatives buy into it; they claim that several people Pablo used to carry out the kidnappings and murders were still alive. The relatives opined that there is no moral justification for the perpetrators to walk freely in the streets of Colombia, actualizing their dreams; meanwhile, they have cut short several others' dreams, so they view it as injustice. Their grouse is not on Luz's effort, but the Colombian justice system with a maximum of 30 years in its penal code for murder; often, the government releases the offenders on parole.

2. *Advocacy strategy*

In this strategy, the root legacy wholeheartedly repents the negative legacy ways and becomes a genuine advocate against it. When the Colombian government sentenced Pablo Escobar to a 5year imprisonment under favorable conditions, common sense should have made him repent completely, serve his deserved sentence, and come out as a genuine advocate against narco-terrorism. Unfortunately, it was not to be; his false sense of power took control of him. I could imagine the impact on Pablo's legacy on drug war if he undertook the following actions:

i)   Complete the 5year sentence
ii)   Dismantle his cartel structures
iii) Co-operate wholeheartedly with both Colombia and American authorities
iv)   Convince other cartel's leaders to abandon the illicit trade
v)   Negotiate a light sentence for repentant cartel members—a motivation for them to surrender to the authorities
vi)   Get involved in the rehabilitation of drug addicts by building rehabilitation centers, especially in the cities where they had sold drugs
vii) Divulge all the tricks in the book used in beating law enforcement agents
viii) Openly and genuinely engage the public through symposiums and interviews on narco-terrorism.

I am convinced that as time goes by, the world would have known Pablo as an anti-narco-terrorism advocate instead of a diehard narco-terrorist. At least, he would have been known as a genuinely repentant narco-terrorist.

A member of a negative family legacy could deploy this strategy as well, but I believe the impact should be more if the root legacy deploys it. The activities of Juan Pablo Escobar, now Juan Sebastian Marroquin Santos, appear to align with this strategy. While he seems genuine in his approach, it lacks the authenticity required to give the much-needed impact as he was only a teenager when his father was at the peak of the illicit trade.

3. Reparation strategy

Reparations are compensations made to victims of a negative legacy or their descendants. The idea of reparations dates back to the 18th and 19th centuries after abolishing the slave trade in Europe and America. There have been ongoing talks on the need to compensate descendants of the victims of the slave trade: African Americans and African countries. So far, no money has been paid for reparations regarding the slave trade.

Concerning World War II, On September 10, 1952, Israel signed a reparation agreement with West Germany in Luxemburg in a solemn atmosphere; Germany started making payments the following year. As of 2008, Germany has paid up to 66 billion Euros to several countries regarding World War II reparations, out of which Israel has received a sizeable chunk: over 25 billion Euros so far.

There is a division of opinions in Israel regarding the acceptance of reparations from Germany; some Israelis call it blood money. In contrast, those advancing the argument for its acceptance opine that the reparations created an avenue to make available the much-needed resources for the economic development of Israel and the resettlement of individual Israeli families.

4. Dissociation strategy

In dissociation strategy, persons connected to the negative legacy surreptitiously dissociate themself from the legacy. Dissociation could include a change of name and location. In my opinion, the strategy appears somewhat self-centered. The dissociation strategy does not address the negative legacy; it only protects the persons that deployed the strategy from the external burden of the legacy. However, certain natural circumstances could place one in a situation, such as marriage resulting in a change of name and location. Nonetheless, I will recommend the dissociation strategy if one's life is in danger following the negative legacy.

After the death of Pablo Escobar, Colombia became unsafe for Pablo's nuclear family; they fled to Argentina with changed identities. Manuela, Pablo's only daughter, still keeps a low profile, and not much of her activities are available in the public domain. Only Juan openly associates with his original name; he is involved in book publishing and reconciliation activities regarding the family's past. Pablo's nuclear family is a classic case of the use of dissociation strategy to good effect.

Nigeria's negative legacy regarding corruption, advance fee fraud, internet fraud, and other inappropriate behaviors are in the public domain. A few bad eggs carry out these activities that impact Nigeria's image globally. I have read several reports of unpleasant treatment meted out to Nigerians in some airports worldwide. When an immigration officer comes across anyone carrying a green passport, the color of the Nigerian passport, their alertness becomes heightened. They subject Nigerian travelers to a more rigorous search procedure than other nationals typically receive. An easy way out is to naturalize to another country with a better reputation through available legal procedures. However, as I mentioned earlier, the strategy only benefits the individual but does not change Nigeria's reputation out there. The action would not have helped the naturalized citizen's relatives, who are still Nigerians. Instead, I will embark on activities that could positively impact Nigeria's reputation than dissociate myself. I know that the criminals who taint Nigeria's image are less than 1% of the Nigerian population. The activities of less than 2 million people should not be louder than that of over 198 million people (Nigeria's estimated population as of 2021 is 200 million). I am not oblivious to the fact that bad news does, however, travels fast.

5. Subsumption strategy
This strategy brought the concept of repairing negative legacies to my

consciousness, and as I probed further, others came to light. Subsumption is a concept where an event or object that is usually smaller is swallowed, absorbed, or overshadowed by a bigger event or object. In subsumption strategy, there exists a negative legacy; however, either the root legacy or those connected to the negative legacy create a positive legacy that can overshadow the negative legacy to the point where the negative legacy becomes insignificant or is forgotten.

In the 2006 world cup soccer final match between France and Italy, Zinedine Zidane, a French footballer, infamously head-butted an Italian defender, Marco Materazzi, in the 110th minute. The action earned Zidane a straight red card and a three-match suspension. There was an outcry from soccer fans worldwide for such behavior from someone regarded as a soccer icon. Despite the infamy, the French public still supported him. Zidane retired from both club and international soccer immediately after the incident (a decision he had made before the world cup). The head-butting and the subsequent sending-off were supposed to be Zidane's last activities in soccer, but he had other plans.

In 2011, Zidane was appointed the sporting director of Real Madrid soccer club, assistant coach in 2012, and Coach in 2016. Between January 2016 and May 2018, Zidane won three UEFA Champions League cups in a row, and within two and a half years of his appointment as Real Madrid's first-team coach: no coach has achieved that feat in the history of soccer. He is also one of the very few coaches to have won the Champions League as a coach and player. Aside from winning the champions league as a player, Zidane also won the world cup with France in 1998, Serie A with Juventus, and several other cups with real Madrid as a player and coach. My son was fifteen years old in 2021; he is a football enthusiast but only knows Zidane's coaching exploits. He knows very little of Zidane's stellar achievements as a player and nothing of his infamous head-butting incident. Zidane has successfully subsumed his infamous head-butting incident with his coaching exploits.

In Zidane's honorable manner, he still served his three-match ban by doing three-day community service in one of FIFA's children's projects since he had retired from active soccer. Not too many people would have deemed it necessary to serve the punishment. My thought is that if Zidane had retired from active soccer after the sending-off incident without coming back to coaching, the negative legacy occasioned by the head-butting incident would have stuck with him like a leech.

Alfred Nobel (1833–1896) was a prolific Swedish scientist and successful entrepreneur. He invented, amongst other things, the dynamite in 1867 that was used extensively for mining and road construction. Unfortunately, the dynamite used for industrial purposes has its unpleasant side; it is a core component for making conventional military artillery and IEDs. Alfred had 355 international patents and established 90 armaments factories during his lifetime, not an inconsiderable feat for an individual.

In 1888, Alfred's brother, Ludvig, died in Cannes, France. A French newspaper mistook Ludvig for Alfred and made a scathing remark about Alfred. In the erroneous obituary reporting, the headline read, "*the merchant of death is dead.*" It further stated that Alfred Nobel made fortunes out of people's sorrows by killing people faster than ever before. The public perception of Alfred's persona may have informed the decision to transfer his assets in his will to form the foundation; it later became the *Nobel Prize*.

In the will, Alfred bequeathed his estate to establish a prize and award annually to anyone that deserves it irrespective of nationality in five categories: Physical science, Chemistry, Medical science and Physiology, Literature, and International Peace. However, owing to the controversies the will generated, legal bottlenecks surrounded the take-off of the award; the family wanted the court to void the last testament of the will that included the prize. In 1901, Five years after Alfred's death, the foundation announced the first set of prize winners.

The initial total assets bequeathed by the will was about GBP 1.7million in 1895; it has risen to $500million according to the Nobel prize foundation in 2020. For each category, the prize money for 2020 was SEK10million ($1.1million). The foundation organizes the award ceremony on December 10 every year to commemorate Alfred's death anniversary.

There are different schools of thought as to why Alfred set up the Nobel Prizes; the motivation behind his setting up the prize is not in the public domain. Since the prize was not in his earlier wills, it gives credence to the argument supporting the French newspaper publication to be the motivation. Currently, few people know Alfred Nobel as the man who discovered dynamite, the precursor to the IEDs, but several people are aware of Nobel prizes for Physics, Chemistry, Medicine/Physiology, Literature, and Peace, including the prize for economics that the bank of Sweden instituted in Alfred Nobel's honor in 1968. My first knowledge of the Nobel prize was in 1986; I was a teenager when a Nigerian literary giant, Professor Wole Soyinka, won the Nobel prize for literature. There was no internet, but I learned about the Nobel prize in my village in then Bendel State, Nigeria. Whether Alfred Nobel deliberately set up the Nobel prizes to repair the negative legacy ascribed to him or not, does not undermine the mileage the prize has gone to overshadow the negative legacy the discovery of the dynamite has inadvertently created.

Between 1976 and 1993, Pablo Escobar strutted the drug underworld like a colossus, making him one of the United States' anti-drug war targets in that period. The Medellin drug cartel, headed by Pablo and the Cali cartel, led by the Orejuela brothers, inundated America and Europe with their daily shipment of drugs. They were also involved in kidnappings and killings in Colombia. When the Colombian forces killed Pablo under controversial circumstances in 1993, the Medellin cartel became fragmented, and the Cali cartel took center stage.

The international nature of the cartels' activities made Cali, Medellin, and by extension, Colombia, acquire a negative legacy. The death of Pablo generated interest globally, and Medellin became a tourist destination, although for the wrong reasons. As soon as the Colombian government restored law and order in Medellin, tourists started pouring in to appreciate the legendary activities of the Medellin cartel. There are a few significant places of interest:

o *Hacienda Naples,* the 7,000 acres fortress that later became Pablo's operational base; it was filled with exotic animals and luxury. The four resident hippos have gone wild and multiplied over the years. As of 2021, over 80 hippos are currently in the wild in Colombia.

o Pablo constructed *Edificio Mónaco,* a six-story building in Medellin's city center for his wife. It was partially destroyed through a bomb allegedly detonated by the Cali cartel; he abandoned it in 1988. In a bid to erase the memories of the Medellin Cartel, the Medellin authorities demolished it in 2019.

o *La Catedral,* the purpose-built prison, was more like a resort than a prison; it was equipped with state-of-the-art amenities for his comfort during the aborted stay in the facility.

According to Federico Gutierrez, Medellin's mayor (2016–2020), Medellin, now dubbed *"The City of Eternal Spring,"* is walking away from its violent past to become an internationally recognized city for innovation, inclusiveness, and sustainability. The authorities decided to destroy Edificio Mónaco, and in its place, they planned to build monuments to remember the victims of narco-terrorism. Medellin's approach is a variant of the subsumption strategy because they want to be associated with a different narrative; nonetheless, they do not want to forget their painful past completely.

Missed opportunities to repair negative legacies

Earlier in this chapter, we saw persons in the path of negative legacy who could turn it around—Zinedine Zidane and Alfred Nobel. We also saw some persons who could not change their negative legacy reputation before their demise: Adolf Hitler, Pablo Escobar, Idi Amin, and Abu Bakr al-Baghdadi. I will examine some of these personalities and identify where they could have taken advantage of opportunities to correct their negative legacies.

In 1991, Pablo Escobar surrendered to Colombian authorities to serve a negotiated five-year prison term under favorable conditions; he built his prison and chose his security detail. One of the conditions was that he should quit all criminal activities. Pablo surrendered and checked into the purpose-built resort-like prison, *La Catedral*, but he did not quit his criminal activities; this led to the Colombian government's decision to move him to a more controlled environment. Pablo escaped from *La Catedral*, and within 16months, he was dead. The *La Catedral* deal was his best opportunity to use his resources and influence to change the narratives. Already, he was stupendously rich and very popular within Colombia; the juicy part of the deal is that it contained a Colombian parliament-backed non-extradition clause to the United States. He should have quietly completed the 5year soft prison term and become a global anti-narcotics advocate. The action would have had a ripple effect in the world of narcotics. Many drug lords or could-be drug lords would have had a rethink following Escobar's action. I am not aware of any attempt by the Colombian government to seize any of his assets during the 5year negotiated prison term.

When Idi Amin seized power from Milton Obote in 1971, he promised his countrymen that he would return Uganda to civilian rule within five years; he ignored the promise. Despite all warnings from the international community through severance of diplomatic relationships with several nations and his ministers' defections, he continued on the path of ignominy. Idi Amin should have set up a local and international reconciliation commission to calm all frayed nerves followed by organizing a free and fair election. During his era, Africa needed a beacon of democracy that would have been a reference point for other African despotic leaders of his time.

From the above examples, it is evident that for those that have found themselves in a negative legacy situation, providence gives them opportunities to retrace their steps if they look deep enough—they also need to have the humility and courage to take corrective actions. I sincerely hope that everyone reading this book that may have found themselves in a negative legacy position can take a cue from this chapter and make amends that would transform them from a pitiable negative legacy situation to a place of positive legacy, positive impact, acceptance, personal happiness, public adoration, emulation, and applause. The pathway is beckoning; unfortunately, it does not last for too long. If the opportunity is not taken on time, the consequences can be dire. Let us be reminded that the negative effects do not end with the root legacy alone; it sticks like a leech and hunts all the connected persons. Imagine a member of the Amin family running for a political office in Uganda, a Hitler running for office in Germany, or an Escobar running for office in Colombia. The burden transcends beyond the root legacy and affects all connected persons' human interactions: social, business, and familial.

How to choose the strategy for best impact

In choosing the strategy that will have the desired effect of repairing a negative legacy, we need to consider some factors:

i. What is the level of legacy? Are you the root legacy or other levels of legacy?

ii. The severity of the negative legacy

iii. The personalities of the people impacted by the negative legacy

iv. Does the legacy impact a group of people, an entire nation, or the world?

Under family legacy in chapter 2, legacy types and levels, Escobar's family legacy was detailed and how it impacted both the immediate and extended family. Depending on where one is at the legacy level, whether the root or family legacy will determine the strategy to adopt. The manner the public will treat a root legacy would likely differ from how they will treat a member of a family legacy. I expect a better show of understanding from the public on a family member than the root legacy.

Another factor is how severe the negative legacy was; for instance, the pogrom of the Jews by Adolf Hitler and the Nazi party cannot carry the same weight as Zinedine Zidane's head-butting of Marco Materazzi in the 2006 soccer world cup match: they do not carry the same weight.

The personalities of the negative legacy victims should be considered. Questions like, do the people forgive easily or not? More work needs to be done to repair the legacy if they do not.

The number of persons affected by the negative legacy is another factor. Is it one person, a few people, a community, the entire nation, or global? Action that can ease or erase a negative impression on a few people varies from steps that need to be taken to correct the image of a country.

Guidelines for choosing a strategy to repair negative legacy

S/No	Criteria	Suggested strategy
1	If you are the root legacy	i. Private/Public admittance and apology ii. Advocacy iii. Reparation iv. Subsumption
2	If you are a member of a family legacy	i. Public admittance and apology ii. Advocacy
3	If the negative legacy affects an individual/few persons	i. Private admittance and apology ii. Reparation
4	If the negative legacy affects a larger group or an entire nation	i. Public admittance and apology ii. Reparation iii. Subsumption
5	If the negative legacy is of a less severe nature	i. Private/public admittance and apology
6	If the negative legacy is of a more severe nature	i. Private/public admittance and apology ii. Reparation
7	If the negative legacy burden bearers lives are in danger following the negative legacy	i. Dissociation strategy

The above is only a guide; other factors could be unique to the circumstance. I view the objective of repairing negative legacy as more of an attempt to right the wrongs as against protecting the root cause or other burden bearers of the legacy. In that regard, the dissociation strategy appears to be more of protecting the negative legacy burden bearers than repairing the legacy; however, it plays an important role in challenging circumstances.

13 LEGACY IN DESPAIR

"Despair is a cruel companion. It robs you of everything; especially the choices that still lie within your control."

.... *Brownell Landrum*

I realized that life does not always work out as expected despite one's grand plans for the future; misfortunes have an uncanny way of showing up unexpectedly. People react differently to setbacks; some face it, weather the storm, and trudge on, while others buckle and devolve into despondency. Hardly will you meet anyone who has never encountered a challenge.

Life's obstacles include poverty, sickness, loss of loved ones, career retrogression, loss of fame and position, loneliness, loss of money, accidents, divorce, childlessness, imprisonment, abandonment, and war. Unfortunately, most of these situations often meet one ill-prepared.

Life's journey is laced with hiccups; our responsibility is to overcome them and come out better. Sadly, several people will despair and act in manners that will not get them out of desperate circumstances. Some may go into alcoholism, drugs, give up on themselves, become a menace to society, become psychiatric patients, and at the extreme, suicide. I will explore the lives of two personalities: Horatio G. Spafford and Joe Biden (the President of the United States as of 2021), to enable us to take some lessons on how to respond to life's adversities.

Horatio G. Spafford (1828–1888)

Horatio G. Spafford was a successful attorney and real estate investor in Chicago, United States. He lost about all his fortune in the great Chicago fire in 1871. Shortly before the fire incident, his only son had died of scarlet fever. After much grief, Horatio needed a break for the family; he planned a family holiday to Europe in 1873. Horatio had to stay back in Chicago because of a business engagement, but his wife and four daughters embarked on the journey. As they were crossing the Atlantic, the ship they were traveling in, S.S. Ville du Havre, had a terrible collision with another vessel and sank in twelve minutes. Over two hundred people died, including Horatio's all four daughters. On landing in Cardiff, Wales, Mrs. Spafford cabled her husband, *"Saved alone, what shall I do?"*

Horatio immediately set sail to England. As they approached the point where the accident occurred, the ship captain, who was aware of the tragedy that had befallen Horatio, showed him where the S.S. Ville du Havre sank. While looking at the spot where his beloved daughters lay, words of comfort filled his heart, and he penned them down.

When peace like a river, attendeth my way,

When sorrows like sea billows roll

Whatever my lot, thou hast taught me to know

It is well, it is well, with my soul

A gospel songwriter, Philip Bliss, rearranged the words into one of the most sung hymns globally. It is difficult to see any choir that has not sung the hymn, often rendered in somber circumstances.

Horatio could have reacted differently. He could have developed nightmares and gone into depression after seeing where all his beloved daughters died, possibly, blaming himself for not joining them on the trip and thinking that perhaps, he could have saved them. He could have jumped into the ocean and committed suicide, yet he penned a hymn that has comforted several people worldwide. Horatio was pouring out his heart in those four lines, but he ended up with a subconscious legacy that has outlived him.

Joe Biden

Born Joseph Robinette Biden Jr., shortened as Joe Biden, is the current and the 46th President of the United States as of 2021. Many will fancy being in his shoes, but life has not always been smooth for the 79-year-old President. Born in 1942, he obtained a law degree from Syracuse University in New York in 1968. In his first marriage to Neilia Hunter, they had three children.

Shortly after being elected to the United States Senate in 1972, tragedy struck through an accident that claimed the lives of his wife, then the only daughter, and seriously injured his two sons. The setback made him consider suspending politics, but he changed his mind and later won six reelections into the United States Senate representing Delaware. He remarried in 1977 to Jill Jacobs and had a daughter with her.

In 2015, tragedy struck again; he lost his eldest son, Beau, to brain cancer. His Memoir, *"Promise Me Dad: A Year of Hope, Hardship, and Purpose,"* aptly describes how he responded to the setback and fulfilled his responsibility to family, country, and the world.

After serving two terms as the United States vice president with Barack

Obama (2009–2017), he became the 46th President of the United States on January 20, 2021. On March 19, 2021, they videoed him falling three times while climbing the stairway to board the Air Force One presidential jet. Going by that incident, many might see him as old and physically unfit to take on the arduous task of presiding over the affairs of one of the world's great nations. Nonetheless, I have a different perception of that incidence. I saw it play out, the reality of man's journey in life, the unpredictable and distressing difficulties that lie along the route. The less than a minute incident encapsulates Joe Biden's personality—a man willing and ready to rise again and again, the daunting challenges notwithstanding. Despite the possible public censure, he gave a salute before disappearing into Air Force One. I saw courtesy, courage, and composure infused in that singular act. Many would have quickly disappeared into Air Force One without the endearing courtesy, away from the censure, at least for that moment.

14 LEGACIES FOR THE SINGLE, SEPARATED/DIVORCED, THE LONELY IN A FOREIGN LAND, CHILDLESS, AND WIDOWED

"Pray that your loneliness may spur you into finding something to live for, great enough to die for."
……………..Dag Hammarskjold

Most singles, separated/divorced, alone in a foreign land, childless, and widowed, will likely have something in common—loneliness. Everyone feels lonely at some point in life, but a prevalent feeling of loneliness harms the individual's physical and mental health. Continuous loneliness could lead to various health risks: increased stress level, withdrawal, depression, anti-social behavior, loss of concentration, cardiovascular diseases, stroke, and suicide.

Experts have suggested several ways to cope with loneliness: connecting with people from your past, reading, joining a club, learning something new, and engaging in a hobby. The impact also varies from person(s) to person(s); some buckle easily under the ensuing stress while others appear to cope better.

In line with Dag Hammarskjold's submission, finding an area of legacy to focus on is another promising avenue to channel one's energies. The physical, mental, and emotional engagements in such causes can take one off loneliness and avoid the attendant risks.

The single

A single is anyone of age that is unmarried or not in an intimate relationship. Singles are particularly exposed to loneliness as they do not have anyone to share private moments. The enforced isolation resulting from Covid-19 restrictions from 2020 up to the present time (2022) has made the situation direr. Until now, outdoor activities such as shopping, clubbing, and the movies were avenues to reduce loneliness; they have either been partially or fully shut down in several countries. The opportunities to meet people physically have significantly reduced; for the few who can brave going outdoors, the suspicion that everyone is a potential Covid-19 carrier makes it more challenging to have close contact with people.

My impression of the singles, irrespective of gender, are people with much to give to an intimate relationship but are yet to find the right partners. The single will have to devise other means of connecting with people because there are people who also need the companionship they crave. I am confident that the opportunities exist, but time and space currently separate them. I enjoin all singles to have that mindset.

The single should also realize that they currently have enough time and resources to give to other aspects of their lives: spirituality, self-development, career/business, relatives, friends and network, neighborhood, country, and the world. If you look at the list above, only the opportunity for an intimate relationship may likely be unavailable for now. Meanwhile, most singles are preoccupied and downcast with the absence of the only one among several opportunities. My take is that the world should not stop because there is a delay in one aspect; instead, the single should carry on the other aspects with enthusiasm. The engagement will help to occupy the single and bring up the other equally important aspects to an appreciable level as you await the intimate relationship.

Areas to leave a legacy for the single

I mentioned earlier that everyone should develop foundational legacies. The singles could leave legacies in several areas. However, I have singled out two foundational legacies: character and network/relationships, along with four non-foundational legacies: knowledge; music, writing, and arts; sports; and humanity/philanthropy.

Instead of brooding over the absence of an intimate relationship, I advise the single to use the period to develop an impeccable character; it will enhance a smooth relationship with the future partner. Use this waiting period to identify, enhance, and reinforce your positive attributes while diminishing your negative attributes. I have seen several cases where people get married after a long waiting period only to separate almost immediately because of irreconcilable differences. If you dig deeper into the root cause of the separation, it will likely be differences in expectations that could be traceable to character. I suggest that the waiting period for the future partner be seen by the single as a *preparation period* rather than a *waiting period*. The more one remains unengaged, the better-prepared one should be for the prospective partner.

There is power in networks; the width and depth of networks deepen with maturity. There are several networking opportunities: high school, college, professional, past and present offices, religious community, clubs, and the neighborhood. It is vital to make oneself visible without being annoyingly loud by being useful, volunteering in project committees, and being accessible. Often, people groups need somebody to drive specific programs; try and take advantage of these opportunities—people are watching. The programs can give the single the visibility needed to meet the future partner. Do remember that he is looking for you just as you are waiting for him; what separates both of you is time, space, and maybe the courage to engage. Recall the descriptors of a well-developed character: courtesy, personable, available, visible, cheerful, positive, supportive, attractive, simple, down to earth, frank, calm, realistic, and faithful. If you imbibe these attributes, your partner is likely around the corner.

One has more freedom when still single; in this period, there is no immediate family responsibility. It is advisable to make the best use of it by developing knowledge in any area of interest. If one does not take advantage of the opportunity during this period, you will likely rue it soon because when the intimate relationship shows up, it will take a chunk of your time. You can acquire a new degree, skill set, write a book, develop a program, or embark on research during the period.

The young singles can go into sport either as a career or hobby; however, the elderly should limit it to a hobby. The proper application of energy and time can get one to legacy status as well as access to different networking opportunities. Sporting activities are also good for both physical and mental health.

Music, writing, and the arts have the unique characteristics of filling the loneliest moments in our lives. Suppose one has a flair for any of them: playing instruments, writing a book, composing music and lyrics, singing, painting, or sculpting; these activities are accessible almost any time of the day and in nearly every location. They can also create networks and audiences for you.

Humanity is another excellent opportunity to engage oneself and have a sense of belonging and fulfillment. If the resources are available, one can fund a cause of interest. One can also volunteer free services starting from your neighborhood. Putting a smile on somebody's face will positively affect you, and it could expose you to beneficial networks. I remember the case of a young lady in my country; she had a flat tire on her way to church on a Sunday morning. A man pulled up to help her change the tire; a year later, they got married.

The separated/divorced

Separations and divorces are rampant worldwide and are becoming an accepted norm; however, they still carry some kind of stigma in some regions. Separation/divorce leaves behind an emotional scar in the heart of at least one of the partners. Some may come out of the relationship eating themselves up for being such a fool to have acted in a manner that caused the separation; others may come out with a self-deluding disposition and heap the blame on the former partner.

Both foundational and non-foundational legacies could help reunite the estranged partners, position one for another shot at a new and enduring relationship, or cope with singlehood. The identified foundational areas of legacy are character, spirituality, and network/relationships, while the non-foundational areas of legacy are knowledge, music/writing/arts, and humanity/philanthropy.

For the separated/divorced, the first goal is to work towards reconciliation. The reason is that aside from the two parties involved, the separation would have caused some discomfort to other stakeholders in the union: the child(ren), the in-laws, and both parties' friends. Often, the root cause of separation is character. A comprehensive review of negative character will help identify the negative attributes that both parties should aim to diminish before taking a shot at a reunion. Suppose a reunion is not feasible; a diminished negative character would be invaluable in the next relationship. If one chooses to remain separated, a diminished negative character could also help in living a more fulfilled life. Excellent character traits naturally endear.

Separation/divorce often leaves emotional and sometimes physical scars on either or both parties. Therefore, the affected party may need psychological support. Spiritual upliftment is a good way of getting such support. Spiritual activities can put you at peace with yourself. Depending on the level of connection, most divine relationships can shield you from the separation's negative emotional impact.

Networks/relationships serve dual purposes for the separated/divorced. The first is the support system; it could fill the vacuum left by the partner. Second, if the separated/divorced intend to take a shot at another relationship, the networks could create the enabling platform. The previous relationship may have been so engaging that one may have inadvertently been inactive in these networks. Do not forget to make your availability known subtly; it is wrong to assume that everyone is aware of your new status.

Pursuing knowledge is another engaging and fulfilling effort. Frequently, separation/divorce creates voids, and the endeavor could fill the emptiness and give other long-term benefits.

Music, writing, and arts could fill the voids in the remotest locations and odd times.

Humanity/philanthropy has the capacity for a tripartite impact on the separated. The first is the fulfillment effect, the second is the engagement effect, and the third is the possibility of opportunities.

Mackenzie Scott is the former wife of Jeff Bezos, one of the world's richest men of the current era. Following their divorce in 2019, she became an instant billionaire after receiving the divorce settlement of 25% shares of the family stock in Amazon. Her estimated fortune was $36billion in 2019. As of 2021, Mackenzie Scott was worth over $60billion, one of the richest women on earth. Scott signed the *Giving Pledge* in 2019, where she undertook to give out a substantial part of her wealth to charity during her lifetime or in her will. Scott's announcement that she was doling out $1.7billion to 116 different causes with no strings attached in July 2020, not even a thank-you letter, redefined contemporary philanthropy's norm that focuses on a particular direction and causes through foundations. Mackenzie Scott is indeed living her life on her terms.

Lonely in a foreign land

I watched a YouTube video of a young, female Nigerian student in Canada, sharing her experiences when she initially arrived. She explained that she was so lonely that frequently, she locked herself up in her room and cried. Relocating to a foreign land has been part of our lifestyle globally. The early settlers in the United States of America were primarily immigrants from many countries, especially Europe. Wars, the quest for a better standard of living, famine, adventure, education, and knowledge are some of the reasons why migrations occur in several regions of the world.

Migration, however, has its initial challenges: culture shock, non-acceptance by the host community, inability to fit into the new system seamlessly, color differences, and language barriers. Those who go abroad alone are inclined to find themselves in lonely situations after leaving their natural support systems: family, friends, relatives, networks, colleagues, and neighbors.

Developing a legacy consciousness can help combat loneliness in such kind of situation as well as avoid rejection from your neighbors. The identified foundational legacies are network/relationships and spirituality, while the non-foundational legacies are knowledge and music/writing/arts.

In networks/relationships, the foreigner should get absorbed in the new society by getting involved in their ways of life. You should understand and assimilate their culture, be friendly and open, and use your skills to good effect. For instance, if you have a good knowledge of cars and find a neighbor stranded, helping in an area as little as changing the car tires can endear you to them.

The initial loneliness should help one grow spiritually. It can also occupy you as well as support your mental health. The beauty of spirituality is that it has no boundaries; you can spiritually connect in the remotest locations.

Knowledge requires time and energy to acquire. The time and the focus to concentrate on a specific knowledge is available during the lonely periods. If the loneliness occasioned by the circumstance is harnessed correctly, it will be more of an opportunity than a challenge.

Writing, making music, drawing, painting, and sculpting are unique areas to develop competencies and engage in lonely situations.

Instead of despair and getting mired down in self-pity, one can turn the challenge into an opportunity. I urge all that have found themselves in such situations to identify and embrace the opportunities through a perception shift and have the courage and motivation to get the best out of the seemingly challenging circumstance.

The childless

There are several causes of childlessness: not being married or in an intimate relationship, the infertility of either of the spouses in a union, and premature death of one's child(ren). The pain of childlessness varies depending on the circumstance. The agony of losing an only child will differ from the despair of someone who never had a child; the latter would have grown accustomed to the situation over time, while the former would be ill-prepared for the shock.

I do not underestimate the importance of help through counseling; however, some legacy areas could also be invaluable in alleviating the effect of the condition. Spirituality, network/relationship, knowledge, music, writing, the arts, and humanity/philanthropy are the identified areas of legacy that could help to lessen the negative impact.

Spirituality can give hope and peace because of its divinity connection. However, it depends on the belief system. Christians believe in Almighty God that can turn any hopeless situation around. Adherents, often referred to as believers, are hopeful of the possibility of miraculous turnaround of events even with the worst medical diagnosis. The psychological impact of the belief system is invaluable.

Being actively involved in networks can occupy one and fill the void a childless situation could create. People in similar situations can create a network in any medium to support and share relevant information concerning their common challenges and interests. I recall a church I visited briefly in Lagos, Nigeria, in 1998. The pastor and his wife were in their forties and were yet to have their biological children. The pastor's wife identified an opportunity to support any member of her church that recently gave birth. She stays with them and supports the woman as if she was the child's grandmother. According to her, that activity always gave her a sense of fulfillment. She further asserted that they are not her biological children but her spiritual children; Christians can relate to this thought line. The lesson from the woman's action is that one can always find a positive place even in dire situations.

Knowledge has the engagement effect; it can also leave you with wealth and a positive legacy.

One cannot underestimate the importance of music, writing, and arts in these circumstances; it offers the much-needed companionship in the home's emptiness. Creating music, writing, and arts provide the opportunity to share your deepest feelings with the rest of the world. However, to achieve it, one should develop the relevant skills.

Philanthropy needs the childless as much as the childless needs humankind. Many childless out there crave to have a child they can cuddle; several orphans, homeless and hopeless children need the love the childless can give. These children are our children because they are the children of planet earth. It is time we changed our perceptions of nurturing only our biological children. Mother Teresa has taught us how to do it. She never married; therefore, she can fall into both the single and the childless. However, she has about the highest number of children globally.

Although my wife and I have three biological children, we are almost getting to the empty nest stage; my wife has planned to adopt two children: a boy and a girl. The great news is that you can decide on the sex, age, and physique of the child you want to adopt; that opportunity is not that available for a biological child conceived through the natural process.

Imagine if all the hopeful mothers, advanced singles, and empty nest families decide to adopt at least one child; how many children would they pull off the streets? The armed robbers, drug addicts, kidnappers, and terrorists that end up as a menace to society are primarily children that were not properly guided and cared for that ended up in the wrong hands. Perhaps one may not be able to care for a child physically; the opportunity to care for children through the financial support of children's homes is there in the form of proxy care.

The widowed

Widowhood is a lonely path no one wants to take, and it is largely unpredictable. One of life's many inevitable challenges is losing a spouse; it often occurs unexpectedly aside from loss through terminal diseases and rarely, execution following a conviction for a capital offense. It leaves the widowed, lonely, hurt, and forced to adjust to the new reality. There could be an increased responsibility to take care of young children alone with lesser income coming into the family. If the primary income earner dies, it will be more distressing for the surviving spouse. There are several legacy areas that a widowed can take advantage of to relieve the grief and loneliness of widowhood: network/relationships, spirituality, knowledge, music/writing/art, and humanity.

The widowed needs support through the existing networks and relationships; it does not matter at what stage of life the loss occurred. The widowed that has overcome the grief can offer support to those that are recently bereaved within the network. It is easier to relate with people who feel or have felt the same pain; sharing common experiences could have a soothing effect.

Spirituality is another excellent avenue to fill the vacuum left by the partner. It connects your inner self to a divinity that lifts you beyond the physical pain. Spirituality can replace despair with hope, turmoil with peace, pain with joy, and anger with pleasure.

Amid the grief and loneliness, pursuing knowledge can be a worthwhile cause. Suppose the demised partner worked on a book project before the transition; the surviving partner can complete the book as a mark of honor and a legacy to the demised partner. The widowed can embark on other personal knowledge acquisition projects; I will recommend this if the desire, time, and resources to follow it through exists.

Music, writing, and art are pleasant companions; I cannot overemphasize the importance of its access to the widowed innermost self and upliftment abilities. Music is lifting and engaging, whether you are a consumer or a music maker. In writing, you can pen down your grief or focus your energies on any topic of interest. Art is another way of letting out your pain as the widowed can depict everything going through the mind in artwork projects: drawing, painting, and sculpting. The paintings can be reference materials in the future.

Philanthropic engagements are another soothing opportunity. The actions should help the widowed to relate and connect with the ideals of the demised spouse. It will also serve as an avenue to honor the deceased spouse. If the deceased spouse was enthusiastic about a particular cause, it would be good to start or continue it.

15 POST-RETIREMENT LIFE AND LEGACY

"Your story is the greatest legacy that you will leave to your friends. It's the longest-lasting legacy you will leave to your heirs."

.............*Steve Saint*

At the end of one's active engagement in any endeavor: religion, business, sports, politics, or government, there will be a point of voluntary, mandatory, or involuntary retirement.

As regards voluntary retirement, one can decide when to quit based on preset personal criteria; you will bow out, watch from the sidelines, and play passive roles: reflection, mentoring, coaching, consulting, writing, and supporting causes of interest.

Mandatory retirement is usually due to age, years of service, or as stipulated by the constitution for political officeholders.

In involuntary retirement, one could retire either due to ill health, redundancy, or change in the political climate.

The opportunities to build lasting legacies are more during one's active life; one would have had executive powers and vigor during the period. In most cases, there will be time to leave further legacies in post-retirement life or repair the negative legacies one might have earlier created. However, the opportunity will not be there in some cases due to ill health, imprisonment, or death.

Recalling Andrew Carnegie's position on the various stages in a person's life, he suggested three phases. The first is to acquire as much education as possible, the second is to make as much money as possible, and the final third, use the accumulated wealth to pursue worthy causes. I believe that Carnegie's advice is more relevant to people in business and a lesser extent, career-based. In acquiring as much money as possible, one should be conscious of the legacy implications because one may put acquiring wealth ahead of positive legacy. Several African countries' politicians and others around the world are classic instances.

I will make a slight tweak to Andrew Carnegie's insightful postulation on the phases of life. Like Carnegie suggested, life should be three-phased; the first phase is education and positive legacy consciousness development. The age range of the first phase could be from birth to as late as forty years; Ideally, it should be from birth to the early twenties.

The next is the career phase, where one has the best opportunity to leave lasting legacies. It could range from twelve years (Andrew Carnegie) to ninety years, as in the case of several countries' presidents that ruled up to advanced ages; some of them died while in office. The former prime minister and later the president of Zimbabwe, late Robert Mugabe, ruled Zimbabwe until he was ninety-three years; the country's military forced him to resign in 2017. Two years later, Mugabe died of natural causes. However, the ideal average age for this bracket should be between the early twenties, after the first degree, until between sixty to seventy years. The retirement age varies from country to country and from profession to profession. The official retirement age is sixty years for public service in Nigeria but seventy years for the Supreme Court judges.

The third and final phase is the retirement phase. The age range of the third phase could be as early as fifty-five years, as in the case of John D. Rockefeller, who retired from active involvement in his business at fifty-eight years. It can also be as late as until death due to old age as with the late Félix Houphouët-Boigny, the former president of Ivory Coast. Houphouët-Boigny ruled the country from independence until he died in 1993 at eighty-eight years. The suggested average age of the third phase is from sixty years until death. At this stage, one may not be involved in activities that could have obvious legacy implications. The level of influence and impact of this stage may be limited, as one's power and influence would have waned. The third phase is the stage for reflection, solitude, coaching, consultation, influencing, persuading, writing memoirs, family engagements, community services, religious activities, and advisory but limited execution. Nevertheless, there are exceptions to the rule, especially when one still has financial power, as in the case of John D. Rockefeller; we will see his post-retirement activities later in this chapter.

The above three-part phase is usually the norm; nonetheless, there is also a two-part variant—limited to those actively involved in their businesses, religious, or political engagements until death. In this case, they will not have the opportunity to reflect on their legacies in retirement. I suggest they reflect on their legacies while still actively building them or during intermittent breaks such as vacations or medical leave.

Medical leave is an excellent opportunity to reflect on one's actions; you will be forced to do nothing other than sleep, read, think, and reflect as one's movement may be restricted, especially if the ailment involves hospitalization. Aside from reflection during medical leave, it is also an excellent period for creativity. For instance, the Automatic Kalashnikov 47, popularly known as AK47, is the world's most used light machine gun and the machine gun of choice of most militaries. Mikhail Kalashnikov, a Russian military engineer, designed the AK47 in 1942 while recuperating in the hospital from the injuries he sustained during World War II. Kalashnikov may never have designed the AK47 if he did not have that time of solitude to think through and design the gun. The machine gun got its name, AK47, from the initials of two words, Automatic, signifying that it is an automatic rifle, and the designer's last name, Kalashnikov. The 47 represents the year the Russian military approved the gun, 1947.

The two-phase variant includes the period of learning and positive legacy development, and execution. The period of execution continues until death. In the Catholic mission, the Pope holds the office until death; it is rare for him to resign willingly or forcibly. Pope Benedict XVI willingly resigned from the papacy in 2013, on account of old age, the first resignation of a pope in seven centuries; the last was by Gregory XII, who resigned in 1415. In the Monarchical system of government, the Monarch rules until death. The beloved Queen of England, Queen Elizabeth II, who also doubles as the head of the Commonwealth, ascended the throne in 1952, over sixty-nine years ago as of 2021, when she was twenty-five years old. She is likely the only Queen of England most of us have known. Barring unforeseen circumstances, she will remain on the throne until she passes on to glory. Félix Houphouët-Boigny, the former president of Ivory Coast earlier mentioned, also falls into the category. The group of people does not have the opportunity to have post-retirement life reflections of their legacies.

This chapter focuses on the three-phased variant where the root legacies have the opportunity to reflect on their legacies. They can either create more legacies or repair the negative legacies created during their active lives. I will review the legacies of two personalities, one from business: John D. Rockefeller, the oil magnate and investor, and the other from politics/government: David Ben-Gurion, one of the primary founders of the nation of Israel.

John D. Rockefeller

I have documented John D. Rockefeller's foray into business and philanthropy activities in chapter 10, *"Wealth or Humanity, which has a longer-lasting legacy?"* As of 1890, Standard Oil, the company he formed in 1870, had grown into a monopoly in the United States' oil industry. Standard Oil controlled the whole oil value chain: crude production, refining, and distribution. Rockefeller's exploits made him a supremely wealthy man; nonetheless, between 1891 and 1892, Rockefeller's workload took a toll on his health. He suffered a nervous breakdown that caused him mild depression, digestive problems, and hair loss in his body that led to baldness. He had to wear toupees to cover his baldness. In 1897, at fifty-eight years old, he retired from the company's day-to-day running and appointed John Archbold to take over the affairs of Standard Oil. As of 1911, when the United States' authorities broke Standard Oil into thirty-four different companies, Rockefeller was no longer actively involved in running Standard Oil. However, the breakup made him wealthier.

Rockefeller either bought into the thinking of Andrew Carnegie regarding the activities one should embark on in each stage of a three-tier phased life, or maybe, it was a coincidence. Rockefeller educated himself early; the ten-week course in bookkeeping he undertook when he was sixteen years in Folsom's Commercial College, Cleveland, is evident. One can trace his business dealings during his active business period from twenty to fifty-eight years of age to his parental influences. Within the period, Rockefeller acquired as much money as he could. After his retirement, the increase in his wealth is more of a combination of providence and the intrinsic value of Standard Oil, which the United States government-initiated breakup brought to the fore. Rockefeller used the third phase of his life to pursue worthy causes of interest. After laying a solid foundation for continuous income flow, he focused on the business of philanthropy throughout the remaining period of his life. Taylor Gates and his son, John D. Rockefeller Jr. (both served as his advisers), assisted him. Rockefeller gave the University of Chicago $75million, Rockefeller University $50million, General Education Board $43million, Rockefeller foundation $235million, and other Universities such as Brown, Columbia, Harvard, and Yale. Rockefeller gave out over $500million to charity during his lifetime. At the time of his death in 1937, at ninety-seven years, the value of Rockefeller's estate was a mere $21 million; he had given out almost all his wealth to charity and his close relatives.

I can analyze Rockefeller's legacy at three levels; the first is the unprecedented manner he revolutionized the oil industry in the United States: drilling, refining, and distribution. The legacy also includes how he deployed efficient management of resources and bargaining power to provide kerosine to the American public at an affordable price. The preceding efforts are essentially positive legacies.

The second level is his predatory business dealings; he used his company's size to chase several competitors out of the market, making Standard Oil a monopolist. The monopolistic status of Standard oil led to the company falling short of Sherman's Antitrust Act of 1890. The breaking of the company into thirty-four separate companies was a direct fall-out of the infraction. Also, Rockefeller's protégée, John Archbold, increased the prices of Standard Oil products leading to a backlash; unknown to the public, he was no longer involved in the running of Standard Oil. The two instances above are negative legacies attributable to Rockefeller.

The third level is his philanthropy activities after retirement; he was so engaged in the activities that one can view it as a job on its own. One cannot underestimate the impact of Rockefeller's third-level activities. Many people may not remember Standard Oil and the infractions that led to its break-up by the government; nonetheless, many will remember Chicago University, Rockefeller University, and Rockefeller foundation. Rockefeller Foundation is still relevant and active in several countries globally; its activities include support in health, poverty alleviation, sustainable energy, disease control, agriculture, education, urban renewal, cultural innovation, and research. Rockefeller's philanthropy gestures have successfully covered the negative legacy of Standard Oil occasioned by the predatory behavior towards the end of the nineteenth and early twentieth centuries. Currently, most people remember John D. Rockefeller for the positive vibes Rockefeller foundation's work has generated worldwide. He is arguably the wealthiest American that ever lived with a net worth of around $400 billion in current times.

David Ben-Gurion (1886–1973)

He was born David Gruen in Plonsk, Poland, then under the Russian Empire rule but later took up the Jewish last name, Ben-Gurion. He was fascinated by Zionism early in his life. Ben-Gurion believed in the return of Israel to their homeland by returning to Palestine. At 20 years of age, he moved to Palestine and worked as a farmer for several years for upkeep but never lost sight of creating the nation of Israel. He adopted the Hebrew name Ben-Gurion while working as a farmer in Palestine. The Turkish governors of Palestine expelled him from the Ottoman Empire during the outbreak of World War I because of his Zionist movement activities. He traveled to the United States and enlisted in the Jewish Legion of the British army following the Balfour Declaration in 1917. The Balfour Declaration was a letter written by Arthur Balfour, the then foreign secretary of England; in the letter, Balfour addressed Lord Walter Rothschild, an Englishman of Jewish descent and a Zionist, where he conveyed the majesty's support for the Jewish ownership of land in Palestine.

Ben-Gurion sailed back to the Middle East to liberate Palestine from Ottoman rule. On getting to the Middle East, the Ottoman Empire had been defeated in World War I, thereby paving the way for Ben-Gurion to continue his long-term objective of resettling the Jews in Palestine. Ben-Gurion pushed for the accelerated movement of Jews to Palestine: he needed the numbers. He founded the *Histadrut*, translated in English as General Organization of Workers in Israel, which later became a galvanizing force for economic, social, and security matters for the Jews in Palestine. He also founded *Mapai*, meaning Party of the Workers of the Land of Israel, in 1930, which he headed. Ben-Gurion later became the chairman of Zionist executives and the head of the Jewish Agency. Following clashes with Palestinian Arabs over the continued influx of the

Jews into Palestinian land, in 1939, the British abandoned their sympathetic policy towards the Jews and supported the Arabs. The British began to restrict the movement of Jews into Palestine; in response, Ben-Gurion organized an international resistance against Britain and formed a Jewish commonwealth in Palestine.

On May 14, 1948, when the British mandate ended in Palestine, supported by the United States and the Soviet Union, Ben-Gurion declared the nation of Israel. The declaration was also in line with the United Nations General Assembly partition plan of November 29, 1947. Ben Gurion doubled as the pioneer Prime Minister and the Minister of defense. He fought off the invading forces from the neighboring countries that wanted to crush the nascent state. He also set the stage for the mass immigration of Jews worldwide to Israel and developed the process of assimilation of Jews from diverse cultures and backgrounds. He instituted the public school system to educate the teeming youths from several backgrounds and cultures.

Ben-Gurion hardline foreign policy stand and his military reprisals for ceasefire violations by neighboring states made him very few friends in the international community.

Ben-Gurion resigned from the government in 1963 and from active politics in 1970; he retired into a hut in Kibbutz, a kind of communal settlement in Sde Boker in the Negev in Southern Israel, to a peaceful life of writing. He wrote an 11-volume book on the history of Israel. Ben-Gurion retired into quietness, appreciated by the nation of Israel for his many sacrifices. He died in 1973 of brain hemorrhage. The Israeli government named several institutions and landmark edifices after him: Ben-Gurion International Airport, the largest airport in Israel; Ben-Gurion University of the Negev, Beersheba; several schools; and streets. His portrait is in two of Israel's currencies: the 500 Lirot and 50 Sheqalim.

Ben-Gurion service to Israel is an ideal example of dedication to a cause and seeing it through. His commitment to the founding of the Israel state is stellar. Hence, Israelis refer to him as the father of the nation of Israel.

He did not retire to luxury; instead, to a quiet hut within the same country, Israel. He was not chased by law enforcement agents into exile but was at peace with himself, having done what he believed was the best for the nation of Israel. His selflessness is worth emulating and should be a case study for political officeholders. As I read through all the commentaries about him, I did not come across any report of corruption charges against him. The only negative legacy he may have acquired over his years of service could be his foreign policy stands that appear hardline and his heavy-handed reprisal attacks on neighboring countries over ceasefire violations.

16 LEGACIES FOR THE DYING

*"We all die. The goal isn't to live forever,
the goal is to create something that will."*

………Chuck Palahniuk

This chapter may appear frightful to several people, but the reality is that we will all exit this earth at some point through death. The expected deaths are in three forms: age, which most of us desire; viruses and terminal diseases; and the death penalty resulting from crime. A few death situations are estimable, while a lot happen unexpectedly. Aside from a few situations where the time of death is reasonably estimable: terminal diseases and death row inmates, we often delude ourselves of not dying so soon, yet every day, we are inundated with reports of deaths worldwide. The focus of this chapter is to explore how those whose death is fairly estimable can still leave a positive legacy behind.

Old age

Old age is not exactly a cause of death, but there are associated sicknesses. Dying due to old age is a dignified way of describing the death of a loved one who has lived to advanced age and transited. Medically, specific causes of such deaths are cardiac arrest, debility, and multiple organ failures. Nevertheless, doctors describe it as *natural cause* because of the associated dignity and the positive impact on the loved ones. At certain ages in life, several organs and systems begin to weaken, and the body may have lost its regenerating ability. A significantly weakened organ or a combination of them could lead to an older adult's death.

Viruses and Terminal diseases

In the last two decades, the world has witnessed several virus attacks and diseases; some are endemic, such as Ebola Virus Disease (EVD) or pandemics (SARS–CoV) of 2002 and MERS-CoV of 2012. The endemic West Africa Ebola outbreak of 2014-2016 spread across Guinea, Liberia, and Sierra Leone; it infected 28,000 people and left 11,000 deaths. Ebola spread to other parts of Africa, Europe, and America, but it was contained almost immediately. The pandemic, Severe Acute Respiratory Syndrome Corona Virus (SARS–CoV), was identified in 2002 in Guangdong, China; it spread to several countries worldwide, particularly Toronto-Canada, Hong Kong, Singapore, Taiwan, and Hanoi-Vietnam. It affected 8,098 people with 774 fatalities. Health officials contained SARS-CoV within one year. MERS-CoV virus that causes the MERS (Middle East Respiratory Syndrome) disease was first reported in Jeddah, Saudi Arabia, on June 13, 2012. It spread to several continents: Africa, America, Asia, and Europe but was more prevalent in Middle East countries (Saudi Arabia, Qatar, United Arab Emirates, Oman, Bahrain, Jordan, Lebanon, Kuwait, Iran, and Yemen), thereby earning the name MERS. According to the World Health Organization (WHO), 2,562 infections in 27 countries that have reported cases of MERS-CoV (Algeria, Austria, Bahrain, China, Egypt, France, Germany, Greece, Islamic Republic of Iran, Italy, Jordan, Kuwait, Lebanon, Malaysia, the

Netherlands, Oman, Philippines, Qatar, Republic of Korea, Kingdom of Saudi Arabia, Thailand, Tunisia, Turkey, United Arab Emirates, United Kingdom, United States, and Yemen). The fatality rate was 35%, amounting to 881 reported fatalities. Saudi Arabia recorded 80% of the infections. As of June 2021, WHO claims that there were no reported cases of MERS; this suggests that the disease has largely been contained.

Human Corona Virus, also known as SARS-CoV-2 that causes the Covid-19 disease, was first reported in Huanan, Wuhan, Hubei province of China; it has spread worldwide and has accounted for the death of over 5 million as of December 2021. Although different companies worldwide have produced several vaccines, the virus is yet to be contained as of 2021.

Before the current era diseases, there have been several epidemics and pandemics worldwide. The bubonic plague of 1346–1353, popularly called the black death, comes tops in terms of the death toll; it was estimated to be around 200 million. It devasted Europe, Asia, and North America. Coming in second is the Spanish flu of 1918, with a death toll of over 50 million. The Spanish flu was first reported in a military barracks in the United States, Camp Funston, in 1918. It is called Spanish flu because of the uncensored reporting of the devastating effect of the flu in Spain; other countries such as the United States, Britain, and France that were equally devastated by the flu were involved in World War 1— their reporting was censored. The plague of Justina comes third in casualty rate; it devastated Europe, Asia, North Africa, and Arabia. The death toll of the plague of Justina was about 50 million. HIV/AIDS, with a death toll of 36.3 million as of 2020, is fourth in casualty rate. The Mexico smallpox of 1519–1520, with a death toll of 8 million, comes fifth.

Interestingly, Mexico's smallpox led to the discovery of vaccines. Vaccination involves using a milder form of a virus to generate antibodies in the body that can fight off the real infection.

Known terminal diseases include Advanced Stage Cancer, Stroke, Dementia, Liver disease, Advanced End-Stage Senescence or Debility,

Adult Failure to Thrive, Amyotrophic Lateral Sclerosis (ALS), and Pulmonary disease.

Capital punishment

The death penalty or capital punishment occurs when the authorities find a capital offender guilty as defined in the state's laws where the offense was committed, and such crime is punishable by death. The death penalty is an old phenomenon; the biblical account exists of three Hebrew men in 600BC: Shadrach, Meshach, and Abednego. They were thrown into a fiery furnace for refusing to worship the God of King Nebuchadnezzar of Babylon. The first recorded codified death penalty was in the 18th century in the code of King Hammurabi of Babylon, where he codified 25 different crimes punishable through the death penalty. Before then, records of executions existed in Britain; methods used for executions then included boiling, burning, hanging, and beheading. Offenses for such penalties were stealing, cutting trees, marrying a Jew, and murder.

The early British settlers primarily influenced the death penalty in the United States; they brought the practice along. The first recorded death penalty in the United States was the execution of Captain George Kendall of Jamestown, Virginia, in 1608, for spying for Spain. Currently, the death penalty in the United States is only murder-related.

In Saudi Arabia, capital offenses that will cause death penalties are apostasy, murder, treason, homosexuality, espionage, terrorism, drug smuggling, armed robbery, blasphemy, burglary, adultery, sorcery, and waging war on God.

In several countries, executions do not follow convictions immediately, leaving many death row inmates unsure when the execution will be carried out. The convicts already know their faith, but the government decides when to carry out the executions. In the United States, many inmates on death row die of natural causes while waiting to be executed.

Possible legacies for the dying

I have cited three instances where one knows that transition is almost inevitable. The only escape route of elongation is a miracle of a turnaround in the health conditions for the two health-related circumstances or presidential pardon for death sentence situations.

In the United States, it is on record that over 10% of death row inmates develop a psychiatric condition known as the *death row phenomenon*; a consequence of the mental/psychological torture they are subjected to by the state before their execution, or in rare cases, pardon. To turn the tide of the psychiatric condition, there is a need to channel the affected person's thoughts into positive actions in the short period they have to live for the common good of humankind. It is achievable by developing a legacy consciousness that will accentuate their self-worth and leave a positive legacy. The assistance of psychologists or mental health professionals may be needed in extreme cases; they are better equipped to manage severe circumstances.

The dying can leave positive legacies in three areas: character, spirituality, and philanthropy.

Character

I defined character in an earlier chapter as unique attributes that individualize a person. I also recognized several character attributes; however, I have identified two attributes that the dying can leave a legacy.

- Integrity
- Openness

In the earlier chapter, I separated integrity from other character attributes to stress its importance, but it does not exempt it as an attribute of character. Integrity is relevant for all three dying categories; however, the death row inmate is singled out here because of the unique circumstance. Often, the convicted may have pleaded not guilty in line with the directives of the defense team during the trial period. If the convicted is still denying the crime but knows that he committed the offense, it will do him and society a lot of good if he comes out clean before the execution. The action will achieve the following:

- Make the convicted be at peace with himself
- Encourage others to tell the truth
- Help the world to know what transpired during the crime
- Help to curb such crimes in the future.

The singular act can leave the condemned with some level of dignity after execution.

Les Brown said, *"The graveyard is the richest place on earth because it is here that you will find all the hopes and dreams that were never fulfilled, the books that were never written, the songs that were never sung, the inventions that were never shared, the cures that were never discovered, all because someone was too afraid to take that first step, keep with the problem, or determined to carry out their dream,"* Les Brown aptly captures my imagination on the quantum of resources that are buried in the graveyard or cremated.

The dying, either through natural causes, diseases, or conviction, owes the world a duty to share their hidden facts, whether in information, secrets, knowledge, or hidden assets. Since they are aware of their possible imminent demise, they can still leave a legacy by sharing such information both for their positive state of mind and for the good of society. As we mentioned earlier, such information dissemination will help the world and make them happier during death. Thus, despite the dispiriting circumstances, they still would have contributed to the greater good of humankind.

Spirituality

Spirituality is one area of legacy that anyone can explore, irrespective of location or circumstances. Even if one is chained to a spot, gagged, blindfolded, or in solitary confinement, one can still engage in one form of spirituality or the order: praying and meditation. I recall years back when the men of my country's special police force arrested me for a trumped-up traffic offense. They seized my phone and transported me to a police station for detention. The only thing I could do was pray for divine intervention; the men were uncooperative. I was unsure of their next action, so I needed a superior being that could control them to intervene at that point.

Despite the desperate situation, spirituality will help to lessen the burden. It will make the person be at peace with himself and support others who are more affected by the unpleasant circumstance. It will give the person the courage to face the imminent challenge. If all death row inmates can increase their spirituality, the chances are that the death row syndrome may not likely occur, or it would reduce significantly.

For the religious groups that believe in life after death, such as Christians and Muslims, the imminent death should bring them joy as they approach the anticipated eternal bliss, irrespective of the circumstances that will cause their death.

Humanity

Despite the imminent reality of death, the opportunity still exists to give back to society.
The dying could have surplus wealth that can fund causes of their choice. Some factors will help suggest the area of human endeavor to fund; personality and life experience should come tops in such factors. The choice of the cause to fund for the aged appears unlimited. However, since aging is a condition that science has not been able to unravel the reversal process, funding research on how to reverse aging is an area that the aged can consider funding.

There are still some diseases that science has not found a cure for yet: Alzheimer's disease, Advanced (lung, heart, and kidney) disease, Cancer, Dementia, HIV/AIDS, Huntington's disease, Pulmonary disease, and Stroke. Applying surplus funds for research into curing those diseases would be a worthy cause.

For those on death row, funding causes for curbing certain crimes or rehabilitating the victims of crimes such as murder, rape, and drugs would be a worthwhile cause as well.

While the above-suggested areas may align with the current life experiences of the people involved, there could be other factors that might have more significant influences on them.

The intent of this chapter is the need for all to realize that there is always an opportunity to leave a positive legacy, no matter how difficult the situation may appear.

I will end this book with the words of Steve Jobs (1955–2011) on his dying bed. Steve Jobs was one of the co-founders of Apple and amongst the most successful tech entrepreneurs of the 21st century who died from complications from pancreatic cancer. His last words were, 'Oh wow! Oh wow! Oh wow!' Wow is a joyous exclamation of admiration or surprise. It is difficult to know whether the exclamation is a function of recollecting his positive legacy-filled life or insight into what lies ahead. Nonetheless, we know that Steve Jobs strove to continue to leave a positive legacy until his dying days, despite his debilitating health conditions.

The End

NOTES AND BIBLIOGRAPHY

Notes

1) When not referring to a specific individual, the masculine gender used throughout this book represents both the male and female gender

2) The capitalization of pronouns regarding God is the standard in Christian literature.

Bibliography

1) Aderet, O. & The Associated Press (September 1, 2019). *In WWII commemoration, German president apologizes to Poland, omits Jewish victims.* Accessed November 25, 2021, from HAARETZ website: https://www.haaretz.com/world-news/europe/in-wwii-commemoration-german-president-apologizes-to-poland-omits-jewish-victims-1.7774400

2) Ahmad, R. (September 8, 2021). *The menace of plastic water bottles.* Accessed November 25, 2021, from EcoMENA website: https://www.ecomena.org/plastic-water-bottles/

3) Al Jazeera & News Agencies. (April 20, 2021). *Chad president Idriss Deby dies visiting front-line troops: Army.* Accessed April 23, 2021, from Al Jazeera website: https://www.aljazeera.com/news/2021/4/20/chads-president-deby-has-died-of-injuries

4) Augustyn, A. (August 13, 2007). *Joe Biden.* Accessed May 1, 2021, from Encyclopaedia Britannica website: https://www.britannica.com/biography/Joe-Biden

5) Bae, H. (April 6, 2015). *Bill Gates' 40th anniversary email: Goal was 'a computer on every desk.'* Accessed May 12, 2015, from CNN website: https://money.cnn.com/2015/04/05/technology/bill-gates-email-microsoft-40-anniversary/index.html

6)   Bar-Zohar, M. (October 12, 2021). *David Ben-Gurion*. Accessed September 03, 2021, from Britannica website: https://www.britannica.com/biography/David-Ben-Gurion

7)   Biography.com Editors. (April 2, 2014). *Andrew Carnegie biography*. Accessed April 8, 2021, from The Biography.com website: https://www.biography.com/business-figure/andrew-carnegie

8)   Biography.com Editors. (April 2, 2014). *John D. Rockefeller biography*. Accessed March 24, 2021, from The Biography.com website: https://www.biography.com/business-figure/john-d-rockefeller

9)   Biography.com Editors. (April 2, 2014). *Mother Teresa biography*. Accessed March 29, 2021, from The Biography.com website: https://www.biography.com/religious-figure/mother-teresa

10)   Business Insider Africa. (December 26, 2017). *How Bill Gates used Microsoft to become the richest man in the world*. Accessed May 12, 2017, from the Business Insider website: https://africa.businessinsider.com/tech/tech-the-rise-of-bill-gates-from-harvard-dropout-to-richest-man-in-the-world/4b678kc

11)   Carnegie, A. (2017). *The Gospel of Wealth*. New York:Carnegie Corporation

12)   Clifford, S. (October 6, 2020). *The inside story of Mackenzie Scott: The mysterious 60-Billion-Dollar Woman*. Accessed May 8, 2021, from Marker website: https://marker.medium.com/the-inside-story-of-mackenzie-scott-the-mysterious-60-billion-dollar-woman-21952a3dc811

13)   Constitutional Rights Foundation. (2014). *The Cold War: How did it start?* How did it end? Accessed November 25, 2021, from Constitutional Rights Foundation website: https://www.crf-usa.org/images/pdf/gates/Cold-War.pdf

14)   Editors of Encyclopaedia Britannica. *Axis Powers* ("n.d"). Accessed October 10, 2021, from Britannica website: https://www.britannica.com/topic/Axis-Powers

15)   Editors of Encyclopaedia Britannica. *Cold War* ("n.d"). Accessed on November 25, 2021, from Britannica website: https://www.britannica.com/event/Cold-War

16)   Editors of Encyclopaedia Britannica. (July 20, 1998). *David Ben-Gurion*. Accessed April 6, 2021, from Encyclopaedia Britannica

website: https://www.britannica.com/biography/David-Ben-Gurion

17) Editors of Encyclopaedia Britannica. (July 20, 1998). *Niani.* Accessed March 31, 2021, from Encyclopaedia Britannica the website: https://www.britannica.com/place/Niani

18) Editors of Encyclopaedia Britannica. (July 20, 1998). *Photoelectric effect.* Accessed April 4, 2021, from Encyclopaedia Britannica website: https://www.britannica.com/science/photoelectric-effect

19) Editors of Encyclopaedia Britannica. (July 20, 1998). *Timbuktu.* Accessed April 1, 2021, from the Encyclopaedia Britannica website: https://www.britannica.com/place/Timbuktu-Mali

20) Editors of Encyclopaedia Britannica. (November 5, 1999). *Nobel Prize.* Accessed April 4, 2021, from Encyclopaedia Britannica website: https://www.britannica.com/topic/Nobel-Prize

21) Editors of Encyclopaedia Britannica. (March 13, 2003). *Al-Qaeda.* Accessed June 23, 2021, from Encyclopaedia Britannica website: https://www.britannica.com/topic/al-Qaeda

22) Farida, F.A. (June 23, 2019). *Reading Nigeria's political history.* Accessed November 25, 2021, from The Republic website: https://republic.com.ng/june-july-2019/reading-nigeria-political-history/

23) Felman, A. (January 31, 2021). *What to know about Coronaviruses.* Accessed October 8, 2021, from MedicalNewsToday website: https://www.medicalnewstoday.com/articles/256521#definition

24) Findlaw's team of legal writers and editors. (June 03, 2020). *Minnesota Second-Degree Murder.* Accessed March 19, 2021, from Findlaw website: https://statelaws.findlaw.com/minnesota-law/minnesota-second-degree-murder.html

25) Gaynor, P. (October 24, 2020). *SpaceX Starship: The continued evolution of the Big Falcon Rocket.* Accessed from NASA SPACEFLIGHT.COM website: https://www.nasaspaceflight.com/2020/10/the-continued-evolution-of-the-big-falcon-rocket/

26) Gordon, J.S. (2021). *John Rockefeller Sr.* Accessed March 23, 2021, from Philanthropy Roundtable website:

https://www.philanthropyroundtable.org/almanac/people/hall-of-fame/detail/john-rockefeller-sr

27) Gregersen, E. (October 7, 2011). *Elon Musk*. Accessed May 12, 2021, from Encyclopaedia Britannica website: https://www.britannica.com/biography/Elon-Musk

28) History.com Editors. (October 29, 2009). World War II. Accessed November 25, 2021, from History website: https://www.history.com/topics/world-war-ii/world-war-ii-history

29) History.com Editors. (October 29, 2009). *Vietnam War*. Accessed November 25, 2021, from History website: https://www.history.com/topics/vietnam-war/vietnam-war-history

30) History.com Editors. (November 9, 2009). *Andrew Carnegie*. Accessed March 29, 2021, from the website: https://www.history.com/topics/19th-century/andrew-carnegie

31) History.com Editors. (February 9, 2010). *Austria's Archduke Ferdinand assassinated*. Accessed March 9, 2021, from History website: https://www.history.com/this-day-in-history/archduke-ferdinand-assassinated

32) History.com Editors. (October 12, 2010). *Spanish Flu*. Accessed September 6, 2021, from History website: https://www.history.com/topics/world-war-i/1918-flu-pandemic

33) History.com Editors. (September 17, 2010). *Black Death*. Accessed September 6, 2021, from History website: https://www.history.com/topics/middle-ages/black-death

34) History.com Editors. (January 5, 2018). *Islam*. Accessed June 28, 2021, from History website: https://www.history.com/topics/religion/islam

35) History.com Editors. (February 27, 2019). *Pandemics that changed history*. Accessed May 2, 2021, from History website: https://www.history.com/topics/middle-ages/pandemics-timeline

36) Kaufman, M.T. (December 9, 1979). *The world of Mother Teresa; Mother Teresa*. Accessed April 2, 2021, from The New York Times website: https://www.nytimes.com/1979/12/09/archives/the-world-of-mother-teresa-mother-teresa.html

37) Kerry, A.D. (April 6, 2021). *Forbes' 35th annual world's billionaires list: Facts and figures 2021*. Accessed August 30, 2021, from Forbes website: https://www.forbes.com/sites/kerryadolan/2021/04/06/forbes-35th-annual-worlds-billionaires-list-facts-and-figures-2021/?sh=151234bc66aa

38) Kiger, P.J. (January 10, 2020). *Six reasons why the Ottoman Empire fell.* Accessed September 3, 2021, from History website https://www.history.com/news/ottoman-empire-fall

39) Lenkowsky, L. *Andrew Carnegie.* ("n.d"). Accessed March 29, 2021, from the philanthropy Roundtable website: https://www.philanthropyroundtable.org/almanac/people/hall-of-fame/detail/andrew-carnegie

40) Linder, D.O. (2017). *The George Zimmerman trial: An account.* Accessed March 15, 2021, from Famous Trials website: https://famous-trials.com/zimmerman1/2319-home

41) Listwa, D. (August 9, 2012). *Hiroshima and Nagasaki: The long-term health effects.* Accessed December 6, 2021, from Center for Nuclear Studies, Columbia University of New York website: https://k1project.columbia.edu/news/hiroshima-and-nagasaki

42) Mclntosh, J. (July 16, 2018). *Fifteen benefits of drinking water.* Accessed April 27, 2021, from Medical News Today website: https://www.medicalnewstoday.com/articles/290814#benefits

43) Klepper, M. & Gunther, R. (December 1, 1996). The wealthy 100: From Benjamin Franklin to Bill Gates-A ranking of the richest Americans, past and present. New York: Citadel Press

44) O'Connor, J.J. & Robertson, E.F. (April 1997). *Albert Einstein.* Accessed July 8, 2021, from the School of Management and Statistics, University of St Andrews Website: https://mathshistory.st-andrews.ac.uk/Biographies/Einstein/

45) Oppel Jr, R.A, Taylor, D.B., & Bogel-Burroughs, N. (April 26, 2021). *What to know about Breonna Taylor's death.* Accessed November 27, 2021, from The New York Times website: https://www.nytimes.com/article/breonna-taylor-police.html

46) Poutanem, S.M. (2018). *Human coronaviruses in principles and practice of paediatric infectious diseases* (Fifth Edition). Accessed October 10, 2021, from ScienceDirect website: https://www.sciencedirect.com/topics/neuroscience/human-coronavirus-229e

47) Rionzi, G. (Summer 2015). *Other nations could learn from Germany's efforts to reconciliation after WWII.* Accessed November 25, 2015, from John Hopskin's University website: https://hub.jhu.edu/magazine/2015/summer/germany-japan-reconciliation/

48) Rotary. Guiding Principles ("n.d"). Accessed November 25, 2021, from Rotary website: https://my.rotary.org/en/guiding-principles

49) Ruth-Ann. *Intimacy and the intimate relationship.* ("n.d"). Accessed November 8, 2021, from Stewart & Associates website: https://counsellingservicevancouver.com/intimacy-and-the-intimate-relationship/

50) Spector, H.R & the Editors of Encyclopaedia Britannica. *The U.S role grows* ("n.d").   Accessed November 25, 2021, from Britannica website: https://www.britannica.com/event/Vietnam-War/The-U-S-role-grows

51) Staff Writer, History101. (January 22, 2020). *Pablo Escobar's wife Maria Victoria Henao hasn't had it easy since his death.* Accessed November 25, 2021, from History101 website: https://www.history101.com/pablo-escobars-wife-maria-henao/

52) State of Minnesota revisor of statutes. *2021 Minnesota statutes* ("n.d"). Accessed March 21, 2021, from Minnesota Legislature website: https://www.revisor.mn.gov/statutes/cite/609.1913)

53) Taylor, A. (October 16, 2011). *World War II: The holocaust.* Accessed October 26, 2021, from *The Atlantic* website: https://www.theatlantic.com/photo/2011/10/world-war-ii-the-holocaust/100170/

54) The Rockefeller Archive Center. *The General Education Board* ("n.d"). Accessed September 5, 2021, from Rockefeller Foundation website: https://rockfound.rockarch.org/general_education_board

55) The Tabernacle Choir (August 2, 2017). *The touching story behind "It is well with my soul."* Accessed April 30, 2021, from the blog: https://www.thetabernaclechoir.org/articles/it-is-well-with-my-soul.html

56) Timsit, A. (October 13, 2020). *The blue print the US can follow to finally pay reparations.* Accessed October 23, 2021, from Quartz website: https://qz.com/1915185/how-germany-paid-reparations-for-the-holocaust/

57) Wood, G. (March 2015 issue). *What ISIS really wants.* Accessed November 25, 2021, from The Atlantic website: https://www.theatlantic.com/magazine/archive/2015/03/what-isis-really-wants/384980/

58) Woody, C. (September 8, 2017). *What the Cali cartel learned from Pablo Escobar, according to a DEA agent who hunted both of them.* Accessed November 25, 2021, from Insider website: https://www.businessinsider.com/cali-cartel-learned-from-escobar-according-to-dea-agent-javier-pena-2017-9?IR=T

59) World Health Organization. *Malaria.* ("n.d"). Accessed April 22, 2021, from World Health Organization website: https://www.who.int/news-room/fact-sheets/detail/malaria

60) World Health Organization. (March 11, 2019). *Middle East Respiratory Syndrome Coronavirus(MERS-CoV).* Accessed October 9, 2021, from WHO website: https://www.who.int/en/news-room/fact-sheets/detail/middle-east-respiratory-syndrome-coronavirus-(mers-cov)

61) World Health Organization. (April 29, 2020). *Salt reduction.* Accessed April 26, 2021, from World Health Organization website: https://www.who.int/news-room/fact-sheets/detail/salt-reduction

ABOUT THE AUTHOR

I have traversed several career paths. My college degree is in business, and I started my career in audit and advisory before moving into banking. After about a decade in banking, I had a stint in consulting before the then minister of agriculture in Nigeria Akinwunmi Adesina swayed me into *agripreneurship*. I have spent about the last decade in the agriculture industry focusing on annual and semi-perennial crops, value chain management, and research.

The desire to share my in-depth and varied knowledge informed my delving into writing and publishing. The publishing arm aims to help newbies and established authors achieve their publishing goals faster, efficiently, and profitably.

Positive Legacy is my inaugural work in the motivational/self-help genre.

I am a minister of the gospel with a focus on knowledge and spiritual empowerment teachings.

I am married to a doting wife and blessed with three wonderful children that keep pushing my desire for success to greater heights.